SO-ARD-813

CANADA

An Introduction for Americans

John Santosuosso

PublishAmerica
Baltimore

First printing

At the specific preference of the author, PublishAmerica allowed this work to remain exactly as the author intended, verbatim, without editorial input.

Quotations from Pierre Berton, *Why We Act Like Canadians*, Penguin Books Canada, 1987, are used with the kind permission of Pierre Berton Enterprises.

ISBN: 1-4241-6505-9
PUBLISHED BY PUBLISHAMERICA, LLLP
www.publishamerica.com
Baltimore

Printed in the United States of America

"We really are quite different from you Americans, even though we talk and dress and look alike."

Pierre Berton
Why We Act Like Canadians

TO JANET

You possess the soul of both the Lily and the Rose

Table of Contents

ACKNOWLEDGEMENTS

Only when I sit down and start to recall all the people who have encouraged my love of Canada do I fully realize just how fortunate I have been. They have given me a gift that I treasure greatly. Reid Lighton, who skillfully served his native Canada, and Marion Salinger, who gave many years of dedication to Duke University's Canadian Studies program, encouraged me far more than either realized. Judith Costello at the Canadian Consulate General in Atlanta helped on a number of occasions. Gerry Foley at the Consulate General in Minneapolis provided assistance on trade information and the activities of the Wheat Board. Mary Ellen Thomas of the Nunavut Research Institute in Iqaluit furnished indispensable insight on Canada's territories. Faculty and staff members at Memorial University in St. John's, the University of Moncton, the University of Toronto, the University of Calgary, and the Canada West Foundation were generous with their time and answered countless questions. The same could be said for numerous Parks Canada personnel at various parks and historic sites throughout the country, and also the staff of several of Canada's major museums.

My lifelong friend, Thomas McIntire, of the University of Toronto, has provided help and assistance in countless ways. Niece Rebecca Pickens Nelson and her husband David have done much to encourage my writing, as have my sisters Lynne Pickens and Jane Ball, and good friends Rosemarie Lamm and Marian Nelson. True sons of Canada, Paul

Pickens and Ian Irving, carefully read the manuscript and did everything possible to rid it of errors. Any remaining ones are solely my responsibility. Jim Styring made beneficial comments on the financial chapter. Prior Smith, of the long-running radio program *Canada Calling*, and Quebec's Judith Isherwood gave encouragement when it was most needed.

My thanks to the Government of Canada for providing the grant that made nearly a month's study in Newfoundland and Labrador possible. Florida Southern College provided several summer grants that enabled me to travel and study throughout Canada. People from one end of Canada to the other, guides, restaurant personnel, taxi drivers, clerks, municipal employees, tourists, and local residents, all shared their knowledge of the country with me, and helped me understand how much there was to learn.

My deep appreciation goes to the staff of PublishAmerica for their assistance throughout the entire publishing process. It is obvious that without them this book could not have been created.

Special thanks go to my very good friend and fellow writer Gary Moore, who knows as much about finance and investments and the ethical standards that should accompany them as anyone in the world. Gary has always been a source of inspiration and encouragement no matter what the topic or situation.

Finally, loving thanks to Pieta, Minnie, and Lady Bug for encouraging barks of enthusiasm. To my wife Janet all my love for her belief in me and my never-ending projects, along with the disruption they create in her home, and for her willingness to share my dreams no matter where they may take me in Canada or the rest of the world.

SOME MATTERS OF STYLE

In order to give the reader as an authentic feeling for Canadian culture as possible, throughout the book the original spelling has been retained for all French proper nouns. However, to facilitate the printing process, accent and similar marks have been removed. I would ask that readers accept my sincere apology for the compromise, made only to make this volume available in a timely manner.

For the most part Canadian and American English use the same spelling. In those few cases where the Canadian spelling for a proper noun does differ it is the one used. Again, the intent is to provide the reader with as much of a Canadian perspective on things as possible. In the instances where it has been necessary to use a word from the language of the Inuit, the meaning is fully explained, and there should be no difficulty in understanding it.

Many may find it helpful to refer to a map of Canada as they explore this volume. Listings Canada has a very useful one at the following website: (http://listingsca.com/maps.asp). The site links with other maps of Canada's provinces, territories, and major cities.

THIS IS CANADA!

The Big Secret

If we think about Canada at all, Americans may have a tendency to take the country for granted. We do know it is up North—somewhere. We may know Canadians do export hockey players and beer. We probably think they must be a lot like we are. Canadians speak English, even most of those who speak French as their first language. Canadians buy and use many of the same products as Americans, read the same magazines, and often make that dream-trip to Disney World.

Enjoy the things we have in common. It can make talking with Canadians and visiting their cities, national parks, and almost everything else they have most pleasant and comfortable. Still, looking at how Canadians resemble Americans is like going out to a five-star restaurant and then eating only half of the dinner. Canada does share a number of cultural attributes with the United States, and also Britain. No nation, including our own, is totally unique. Yet, there are many characteristics of this magnificent country that are distinctly Canadian, and which far too often are a national secret that never gets beyond the country's borders. So, be ready to be surprised, as you take a close look at the country that is Canada. In the pages ahead, we will explore not only what it actually is to be Canadian but also why this land is of critical importance to the United States, and indeed the world. Finally we will offer some impressions of places in Canada even some Canadians overlook, and provide insights into Canadian history, politics, and economic matters. Get prepared for a surprising journey.

An Economic Heavyweight

Pay attention to the financial news very long and most certainly you will come across items on American trade relations with Japan. Perhaps you may also hear about our growing trade, and deficit, with China. Everyone knows we have to pay attention to the European Union these days. Obviously all of these places impact in a major way upon America's financial health. It often comes as a surprise to discover that our trade with Canada is greater than with any other country. The Canadian market has always been America's largest, even before the establishment of the North American Free Trade Agreement (NAFTA). Daily the two countries exchange goods and services valued at over two billion dollars. Somewhat more amazing is the discovery that our trade with Canada's most populated province, Ontario, alone is larger than that which we have with any country other than our total commerce with Canada. Quebec, Canada's French-speaking heartland, is another key player in our country's international trade, buying and selling more in the American market than all but a handful of other trading partners. Clearly, Canada's financial health is vital to the United States. Quebec Hydro, the giant electricity producer, is a major player in the energy market of the Northeastern United States. Without the oil and natural gas that flow out of the western province of Alberta, we would be drastically more dependent on energy sources much further from home and in lands much less stable. Canada is now our largest supplier of imported hydrocarbons. One of Canada's most visible corporations, Nortel, supplies critical technology to many American firms. Its presence is so strong here that many people believe it is actually an American company. Great West Life Insurance Company, with its headquarters in Winnipeg, Manitoba, furnishes group health insurance for American workers. Meanwhile Canada is an excellent customer of many American businesses, both large and small.

There are other venerable Canadian firms that have played a vital role in the history of our continent. The building of the Canadian Pacific Railway was an essential step in the creation of Canada as a nation, linking it from the Atlantic to the Pacific Ocean. If you ever spent a romantic evening at the luxurious Hotel Chateau Frontenac in Quebec City, or marveled at the unforgettable beauty of the Canadian Rockies through a window of the majestic Banff Springs Hotel in Alberta's Banff National Park, you have enjoyed one of the world-class establishments long carefully managed by Canadian Pacific, Limited, along with its rail, shipping, and energy operations. Events in 2001 led to the creation of five different companies out of this venerable corporation. As a result, future success probably will be even greater.

The Hudson's Bay Company, affectionately known as The Bay in Canada, first opened its doors in 1670 and has continued to serve its customers ever since that time. It is the world's oldest continuously operating company. King Charles II of England granted the company's original charter, and in 1970 it became a Canadian corporation with headquarters in Winnipeg.

Although most people associate The Bay with the fur trade, land sales, and remote northern trading posts, today it confines itself to running upscale department stores in Canada's largest cities, such as Toronto, Montreal, and its flagship operation in Winnipeg. Smaller outlets are in resort areas such as Banff and Lake Louise. Many former Hudson Bay stores in the far North still serve customers in areas where accessibility is often rather limited, but today the North West Company is responsible for their operation. It purchased the locations from the Hudson's Bay Company in 1987. Northern Stores provide nearly everything including groceries, television sets, and washing machines to residents of communities who depend on them for both the necessities and comforts of life.

Trading with the World

The future for Canadian-American trade should be bright, as both nations are actively seeking to increase it. Along with Britain, Japan, Germany,

France, and Italy, Canada and the United States attend the semiannual meetings of the G-7 (G-8 when Russia attends) nations. The meetings serve as "economic summits" where these states make financial decisions they hope will stabilize world currencies and advance the global economy. In 1989 Canada and the United States entered into the Free Trade Agreement to work toward the elimination of tariffs on goods they imported from each other and to provide a mechanism to assure fair and reasonable entry into each other's markets. Mexico joined in 1994, thus creating the North American Free Trade Agreement, or NAFTA. Canada has a similar treaty with Chile, which could ultimately pave the way for that nation and additional states to become NAFTA members. Obviously the Canadian presence is welcome in the promotion of international trade and commerce.

Certainly not all trading relations between Canada and the United States are harmonious. Canada is definitely not the United States. Like every other country in the world, it pursues what it perceives to be its own best interests. These sometimes conflict with those of America. Despite an international treaty, which was supposed to resolve the dispute, seemingly every year the salmon fishermen of Alaska and British Columbia quarrel over fishing quotas. American grain farmers sometimes are in vigorous competition for various markets with those of Canada's Prairie Provinces. In an attempt to protect its publishing industry and deter what it sees as a threat to Canadian culture, the federal government has passed legislation to limit American content and advertising in Canadian magazines. Even the Canadian Football League, whose rules differ from American football, requires teams to carry a quota of Canadian players! This is what one should expect from a people who comprise a fully sovereign nation. Canada on one occasion seized a Spanish fishing vessel for allegedly fishing in Canadian waters, but on the whole this is a country that has a reputation for cooperation and dealing fairly in international trade.

A Reliable Ally

To the surprise of many Americans, in the nineteenth century, Canada sometimes saw the United States as a diplomatic and military adversary.

The twentieth century has been quite the opposite. Canada and the United States were close allies in both World Wars I and II. Some Americans even enlisted in the Canadian armed forces during World War I before the United States entered the conflict in 1917. Canadian troops also fought in the Korean War. The two nations were among the founding members of the United Nations and from the start have been supporters of the North Atlantic Treaty Organization, the Western defense pact better known as NATO. Peacekeepers from Canada have participated in the effort to stabilize Bosnia. Canada took part in the Desert Storm operation for the liberation of Kuwait, and it rapidly came to the diplomatic and military support of the United States after the September 11, 2001, terrorist attack on the World Trade Center. Differences over war in Iraq are real, but there is absolutely no doubt that the two countries remain committed allies.

Canada's Arctic and sub-Arctic North contain relics of the Cold War that are reminders of joint American-Canadian projects to provide warning and defense in the event of Soviet invasion across the North Polar regions. In 1997, on a trip to Labrador, near the coastal community of Cartwright, I managed to spot a still-standing tower which had once been part of the DEW Line, the Defense Early Warning System, intended to detect any Russian missiles before they reached targets further south. Happy Valley-Goose Bay, Labrador, has long been the home of a thriving NATO airbase, currently used for low-level flight training. Although some of the activity may now be on the way to being phased out, in recent years the pilots have been more likely to be German, Italian, Dutch, or British, but you may see a few Canadians or an occasional American as well.

Just outside the northern Manitoba settlement of Churchill, on the shore of Hudson Bay lie the ruins of a joint Canadian-American military base, which was a temporary home for several thousand personnel. Today it is no longer needed and is essentially abandoned. However, one Quonset hut has been converted into the infamous "polar bear jail," where Churchill's best known residents, should they wander into town looking for a meal, are housed until the bay freezes in November. Then they can be released on to the ice to indulge in seal hunting, which is what Nature intended them to do, rather than raid the town dump.

Perhaps Canada's cultural differences from the United States accounted for its long reluctance to join the Organization of American States, the OAS. Headquartered in Washington, the OAS was strictly for the United States and its Latin neighbors, as far as Canada was concerned. When some of the English-speaking island nations of the Caribbean decided to join, Canada finally took a similar step and became a member in 1990. In view of the fact that the border between the United States and Canada was for many years the longest unfortified one in the world, it seems appropriate that both nations should be working together in the organization that focuses on the needs and concerns of their part of the planet.

Tourism

Today Canadians own more property in Florida than citizens of any country outside the United States. It is not unusual, especially in the winter time, to see Florida hotels and trailer parks flying the Canadian flag or hear the long-running program *Canada Calling* on the state's radio stations. Several Florida weekly newspapers publish for Canadian visitors during the winter months. Similar situations exist elsewhere where Canadian winter visitors migrate.

In the summer the situation is partially reversed with Americans flocking to the Canadian Rockies, touring the only walled city in North America north of Mexico, Quebec City, and perhaps seriously considering buying vacation property in Nova Scotia. Outdoor sportsmen love the mountains, lakes, and wilderness of the Canadian North throughout the year. Tourism is big business for both the United States and Canada. Each country contributes significantly to the success of the other in that industry. Canadians have even endured the burden of a stronger United States dollar and an unfavorable exchange rate to venture south, as they did to show their support for New York City in its struggle to recover from the September 11th tragedy. If they stopped coming they would be deeply missed. Now, as their currency has strengthened, they should play an even more vital part in America's vital tourist industry.

A Multicultural Society

Proving that multiculturalism can work may ultimately turn out to be one of the greatest contributions Canadians make to world affairs. French Canadians, in particular, have long liked to talk about the "two solitudes," the fact that two different cultures, the English and the French, are the foundation for Canada since its creation. The aboriginal peoples (the term used in Canada's Constitution), consisting of Indian bands (they prefer that term rather than "tribe") and the Inuit (the correct name for the Eskimo) claim they are just as much distinct cultures as the French or the English. Although they comprise a percentage of the total Canadian population not much greater than the Native American does of the United States, in large portions of the sparsely populated North they are a decided majority and most definitely have left their identities upon this region. They have also helped shape the society of the more heavily populated southern portion of the country.

The Metis are little known outside Canada but have made yet another contribution to Canadian multiculturalism. They are the descendants of the French Voyageurs, the fur traders and trappers who played the key role in exploring and settling Canada's interior, and their Indian wives. While found throughout all of Canada, the largest concentration of the Metis is in the Manitoba capital of Winnipeg, particularly in the section which once comprised the separate French city of St. Boniface. The Metis are justly proud of their culture and try to maintain it along with their own distinct dialect of French. Of course nearly all are also comfortable in the mainstream culture of the country and are bilingual.

Undoubtedly the greatest of the Metis heroes is Louis Riel, who lies buried in the cemetery of St. Boniface Cathedral. Riel was educated in Montreal but born in St. Boniface on the Red River. As the Metis leader he played a part in bringing about the 1870 agreement that brought the province of Manitoba into the Canadian Confederation, along with special rights for the French and Metis . Sadly, his life had a tragic ending, to which we will return later.

Although these may be considered the "founding nations" of the country, numerous others have come and left their mark, helping to create a land that is as diverse and vibrant as any. North of Winnipeg at Gimli, Manitoba, is the largest settlement of immigrants from Iceland anywhere in the world. From the Red River, as it flows by Winnipeg, you can easily spot a large onion-domed structure, the Ukrainian Orthodox Cathedral. It is an appropriate symbol of the early twentieth-century immigrants from the Ukraine, Russia, and elsewhere in Eastern and Central Europe who were attracted to the rich farmlands of the Canadian prairies, not only in Manitoba, but also in Saskatchewan and Alberta. Even the Americans are here, many having settled in oil-rich Alberta, the province some say does resemble the United States more than any other.

More recently immigrants from other places have been arriving. Haitians feel an affinity with Montreal because its French language and culture give them some linkage with their Caribbean homeland. On a trip to Toronto I visited an inner city "immersion school" where English-speaking children were taught entirely in French. Approximately forty different nationalities were represented in the student body. At least for some, English was their second language, and now French was their third. More than one out of three residents of Toronto is now classified for census purposes as a "visible minority," which in most instances means Asian.

Western Canada is no exception. Vancouver, the country's third largest city, and its Pacific-Rim port, has a very large Asian population. In the interior you may find a smaller but significant number in booming Calgary, and do not be surprised if your taxi driver in Winnipeg may have come from some place such as Bangladesh. Canada has been a popular destination for immigrants from the various parts of the Indian subcontinent.

The amazing thing about this tremendous variety of people, languages, and cultures is that it does seem to work. To say there is no racial or ethnic tension in Canada would of course be incorrect, but given the cultural mix the amount is amazingly low. If Canada can make multiculturalism a success it may have a tremendous advantage in this age of the Internet and the global economy, when the entire world is your marketplace.

A Sign of Things to Come?

Former Indiana Congressman Lee Hamilton, while a member of the House of Representatives, had a reputation for caring about Canadian-American relations. A report by L. Ian MacDonald, appearing in the September 25, 2000, edition of the Montréal *Gazette,* noted that Hamilton as director of the prestigious Woodrow Wilson Center in Washington was seeking to promote Canadian studies at the center's location in the Ronald Reagan Building. The center is intended to be a place for both scholars and politicians. It does not devote all its attention to Canada, but upon taking command, Hamilton made it clear that it would have a solid Canadian program, and the Center has established a Canada Institute. From the diplomatic, strategic, and economic points of view, Canada is too important to ignore. Several major American universities, including Duke, the State University of New York (SUNY), the University of California, and the University of Washington have highly-regarded Canadian Studies programs that promote both research and teaching about the country. If Americans forget about Canada, they will have lost as many opportunities as Canadians will. As the century progresses the need these two nations have for each other should not diminish but grow stronger.

STOPPING THE STEREOTYPES

Don't Bother to Add a Star to the Flag

If an American really wants to annoy a Canadian, the best thing for him to say is, "Why don't you become the fifty-first state?" Some replies we better not print here. The most gentle response is apt to be, "Why don't you become the eleventh province?" Generally, Canadians like Americans, but they are not Americans. They are proud of the differences.

It is not so much that they see things wrong with America. Rather, it is they are proud of some of the things they sense are Canadian. Popular Canadian writer Pierre Berton, in his book *Why We Act Like Canadians,* remarks that this is "a land of peace, order, and strong government." Indeed it has been and still is, even if in recent years some of the governmental emphasis has shifted from the federal administration in Ottawa to the provinces. Most Canadians welcome certain things many Americans would not. They are pleased with their National Health Care plan, and are quite willing to shoulder a higher tax burden to pay for it. They know it is not perfect. There is almost always some discussion about the desirability of privatizing at least parts of it. Stories of Canadians coming south into the United States to seek an alternative are true, but for the most part it delivers a very good product, and, unlike some Americans, Canadians are not likely to slip through the cracks and have no coverage. One of the things that binds the nation together is this high level of concern for the general welfare of all its citizens.

The love of peace and order probably has some of its roots in the early settlement of the country. In Fredericton, the capital of the province of New Brunswick, while walking along the bank of the St. John River one rather cool October morning, I came across the crumbling ruins of what were largely illegible but quite clearly grave markers. They were all that was left of the original Loyalist cemetery. The first English-speaking settlers in the area came here because they wished to remain loyal to the British Monarch, and they wanted nothing to do with revolution against the mother country. In many instances their allegiance cost them their lives. Most would perish during the first winter. Nearly all of the early English inhabitants of Ontario were also Loyalists who left the rebellious thirteen colonies rather than rebel against George III. Along the shoreline of Lake Ontario are a number of communities still very proud of their founding by United Empire Loyalists.

More Than Moose and Mounties

I must admit I have only ever seen one moose roam free in Canada. She was quietly grazing along the side of the highway, near Gander, Newfoundland. As I rode slowly by we took a casual look at each other and then each of us went quietly about out business. Of course there are a lot of moose in Canada. Terra Nova National Park in Newfoundland even has a sign warning motorists to be careful and indicating how many moose-related automobile accidents there have been so far during the year. Nevertheless, for the most part if you want to see moose in Canada, it is a situation like searching for bears in the United States (Canada, of course, also has those). You may occasionally spot one near a populated area, but usually you are going to have to go into the wilderness areas to find them. Canada has a rich treasury of wildlife. Canada also has sophisticated urban areas where the only wild life you are likely to see is someone wearing the latest fashion styles. Walk through downtown Toronto's glass-enclosed Eaton Centre, Montreal's massive underground shopping areas, or the world-class West Edmonton, Alberta, Mall, with its amusement and water parks, and you soon realize that Canadians do not lack the comforts of the city.

As for that other symbol the Mounties, well, yes, they are real, but few wear broadband hats and scarlet coats. Those are fine for parade duty, but the Royal Canadian Mounted Police have from their start in 1873 been well trained and effective federal law enforcement officers, and you normally will find them wearing much less flashy but far more serviceable uniforms. They do not act like the shy, somewhat naive characters you sometimes see in film or on television. In the Northern territories, they are the sole law enforcement agency, and in all provinces except Ontario and Québec (which have their own forces) function as the provincial and criminal police. Throughout the entire country they are responsible for internal security, a role quite similar to that of the FBI in the United States. Of course Canada does have other less known, but just as resourceful, law enforcement personnel as well. Larger municipalities usually have local police services. In Newfoundland and Labrador the Royal Newfoundland Constabulary has certain responsibilities. For many years it was proud of the fact that officers did not carry weapons, although they were authorized to keep them in the trunks of their vehicles. In the summer of 1997 that finally had to stop, and I recall for the first time seeing the police patrolling St. John's, the capital, on their bicycles and with their revolvers. It was a sad thing, but even in law-abiding, peace-loving Canada things have changed. Today no Canadian prime minister would probably dare to imitate former Prime Minister Pierre Trudeau who used to go out alone for a ride on his motorcycle.

Canada is proud of its relatively low crime rate, but every country feels the stress of modern urban complexities, and the pain that rapid change often brings. The result of these situations is all too often more crime and violence, and no country, including Canada, should expect to be an exception. Still, one of the enjoyable things about Canada is the fact that for the most part its streets are safe and you can spend your time exploring what you see rather than worrying about crime.

O, To Be in England?

On one occasion I attended a Sunday morning service in the Anglican cathedral in St. John's, Newfoundland. Although Europeans probably discovered and settled in Newfoundland earlier than any other place in North America, the province of Newfoundland and Labrador was the last to join the Canadian federation in 1949, after a very close vote the previous year. So, it is not surprising to find some strong emotional ties with Britain still linger here. The British Union Jack was rather prominently displayed near the front of the church's chancel. After the service concluded I went looking for the Canadian Maple Leaf flag I felt must be somewhere here. I finally came across it—much further back, and much more difficult to see. Perhaps this proves absolutely nothing. Maybe the British Union Jack was always displayed where it is now, even before 1949, when Newfoundland was not part of Canada. Probably it does indicate these folks are proud of their British heritage, but it does not mean they are not good Canadians.

My wife has had for many years a rather worn photograph of Queen Victoria. She received it from a friend who has Canadian ancestry in part of her family. The picture is very typical of those you often found around the end of the nineteenth century in nearly every home in those communities with United Empire Loyalists roots. Although you would not be likely to come across this now, I have been told that at the time even an occasional French Canadian family might have such an item. It is difficult to imagine a symbol more appropriate of the linkage between Canada and Great Britain. Of course today Queen Elizabeth II is Queen of Canada as well as of the United Kingdom of Great Britain and Northern Ireland. As such her portrait appears on all Canadian coins and many banknotes. Nevertheless, portraits of British monarchs tell only part of the story. Most Canadians have a fondness for Britain, but they are not British.

This becomes very clear when you look at aspects of their government. Yes, both countries have a Parliament, and the lower house in each case is the House of Commons. However, no one in the upper house, the Canadian Senate, ever possessed an inherited title of nobility, as they did until recently in the British House of Lords. Like the United States, and unlike Britain, Canada has a federal form of government with constitutional power divided between the provinces and the federal government with its capital in Ottawa.

We have already remarked that Canada is the land of the "two solitudes." Its French culture is something you would not find in the British Isles. While the heartland of this is Quebec, it certainly is not limited to there. In Canada's smallest province, Prince Edward Island, residents who are proud of their French Acadian heritage sometimes fly the Acadian flag, which is similar to the French tricolor with a gold star added. The Acadian settlers of Canada's Maritime region on the Atlantic coast were among the very earliest of European colonists to come to this land. Nova Scotia was their original home. Later those who escaped expulsion to Louisiana by the British made their way to Prince Edward Island and New Brunswick. Approximately 31 percent of New Brunswick's inhabitants speak French as a principal language in their households, and the province enjoys a unique bilingual status under the Canadian constitution. In the West the Metis have left their own distinct French culture on parts of Manitoba.

Of course the native peoples, both Indian and Inuit, have also shaped Canadian culture. In the far North they are dominant, but their presence is also felt in the southern and more heavily populated parts of the country, along with more recent immigrants from many lands who decided to make Canada their home.

The years have taken all of these cultural contributions and blended them into something that is often difficult to define or describe. It really needs to be encountered and experienced. Only then do you begin to comprehend its vitality and the fact that it is truly and uniquely Canadian. Indeed, Canada has been shaped by its people, its history, and its geography into something that to a certain extent may be elusive, but which is dynamic and vibrant. Now it is time to take a closer look at what these forces have created.

O CANADA

Even many people who know little about Canada are familiar with its distinctive National Anthem, *O Canada*. Among its lyrics are the stirring words, "The True North strong and free!" It is indeed all of those things, and many more, for this is a country blessed in many ways. It is a land of great diversity, both in people and resources, and that is the key to its richness.

True North

Part of the national mythology is that Canada's location in very northern latitudes has helped to create a hale and hearty people who know how to survive in any adversity. There may be some truth to this. Only resourceful people are likely to successfully challenge the rigors of an Arctic winter. On the other hand, the Canadian landscape is a rich diversity and by no means entirely Arctic. Ontario's Point Pelee, the most southern spot on the Canadian mainland, lies at a latitude similar to that of northern California. The most heavily populated part of Canada is that found in the southern Ontario peninsula and on up into Quebec's St. Lawrence Valley. This is an area that is further south than some of the United States. Minneapolis and Seattle are further north than Toronto or Montreal. Victoria, British Columbia, a short distance west of Seattle, enjoys a mild climate thanks to the Japanese Current in the Pacific Ocean. It is a popular city for retirees, with only occasional snow, and where golf is possible much of the year.

Canada also stretches literally across the North American continent. St. John's, Newfoundland, one of the oldest cities in North America, actually is closer to Ireland than it is to Winnipeg in Canada's prairie heartland. Grise Fiord, in the Inuit Territory of Nunavut, is one of the most northern-inhabited communities in the world and is some 2,000 kilometers northwest of the territorial capital of Iqaluit, which itself is 2,100 kilometers north of Montréal (Canada, like most nations, uses the metric system more than the English system of weights and measures; a kilometer is approximately five-eighths of a mile).

In addition, the terrain provides an almost endless variety of landscapes. Except for some peaks in Alaska, the Rocky Mountains in the Yukon Territory are North America's tallest. In contrast, the prairies are so extensive that Indian legends claim a man could stand at a particular point to watch a buffalo herd pass by, and it would take three days before the last animal went past his spot. Great Slave Lake, in the Northwest Territories, is among the largest in the country. I remember flying over it once on the way to Japan. At first not knowing where I was, I thought in amazement we had reached the Pacific Ocean much earlier than I believed possible.

Off the coast of Labrador is "Iceberg Alley." This is a place made more popular since the release of the film *Titanic.* Stand on the deck of a ship here and you will get tired counting the icebergs flowing south through the Labrador Sea into the Atlantic Ocean. Here the journey that began when they broke off from the Greenland Ice Cap finally ends, as they slowly melt away. There is also the rugged beauty of the Canadian Rockies in the country's national parks, including such famous ones as Banff and Jasper in Alberta, but also the seldom-seen wonders of what must be the world's most remote one, Ellesmere Island, which lies west of the most northern areas of Greenland. The splendors of this land are almost infinite.

The World Meets Here

Her people are as diverse as her geography, probably reflecting that this has been a welcoming land, and one that offered great opportunities, but not easy ones. What kind of ethnic food do you want to try? You are certain to find it in Toronto if it exists anywhere. Journey through the little town of Veregin in eastern Saskatchewan and you will discover a few lingering structures that are reminders of the fascinating people who first settled in this community, named in honor of their leader, over one-hundred years ago. In 1899 the Doukhobours, pietistic Russian immigrants, came to Canada seeking both freedom and farmland. If they felt their liberty or rights were threatened, they had an effective way of protesting. They would simply take off their clothes! Hutterites from Germany were not prone to demonstrating naked but ventured forth to the Canadian prairies for the same reasons, religious freedom and land.

Of course we have already mentioned the "founding peoples," the French, the English, and the native groups such as the Cree, Dene, Inuit, and others. Clearly one can speak of the "two solitudes," for Canada's English and French roots are deep and strong. If at times they create tension in their effort to coexist, they also produce a distinctive richness that makes this nation truly unique. Yet there is more. As others came in later years they added their own contributions. Today the result is a people that in many ways are like no other. They are genuinely Canadian.

A People Seeking to Confirm an Identity

But the story is something far more than some sort of travelogue. It goes much deeper than that. When Bernard Landry, seeking to lead the Parti Quebecois and thus serve as Quebec's provincial premier as well, made remarks in French which apparently were misinterpreted as referring to Canada's distinctive red maple leaf flag as a "red rag," there was an immediate reaction from the province's population. Support for Quebec sovereignty underwent a significant drop. One cannot help but wonder if many a *habitant* (resident), is unhappy with Quebec's situation within Canada, in fact unhappy enough to leave, but at the same time feels a certain undefined love for the country and a longing to be fully part of it. There is a search for dignity, a desire to stay, but a refusal to do so unless there is total acceptance of who they are and always have been.

English Canada also must find itself with certain ambivalent feelings. The symbols are still there. The Queen's portrait is usually on the nation's currency, but since 1952 her official representative, the Governor General, has always been a Canadian and has been selected by the Canadian government since 1936. The national anthem, *O Canada,* is far more likely to be heard than *God Save the Queen.* While love and respect for the monarch remain, now you are less likely to find her portrait in English Canadian homes, where once Queen Victoria's was almost an essential furnishing. Today no Canadian government would automatically think of following Britain's foreign policy any more than it would America's, although it is a loyal ally of both. There is pride even in a beer commercial which stressed what it is to be Canadian. Exactly what that may be is an elusive concept, still difficult to define, and without total agreement on the contents, but there is strengthening consensus that it is real and deeply meaningful.

The Ribbon of Steel

Perhaps it is quite appropriate that Canada was born of the railroad, and for its first century it was the railroad as much as anything that bound the country together. Those steel rails are a powerful link, yet a thin one. They are a symbol of both the strength and the fragility of the Canadian experiment with nationhood. When British Columbia was asked to join the Canadian Confederation in 1870, its price was the Canadian Pacific Railroad, which finally was completed in 1885. Not only would it link the Pacific Coast with the Atlantic but it would open up the prairie interior to sometimes desperate immigrants seeking land, religious toleration, and a future. Even the Maritime Provinces found a railroad helped make the idea of Confederation more palatable with its possibilities for greater commerce with Quebec and Ontario. The privately owned Canadian Pacific network would manage to coexist with the government-operated Canadian National, along with small, often exotic sounding lines such as the Algoma Central and Hudson Bay or Vancouver Island's Esqumalt and Nanaimo. The rails would serve the same purpose as the earlier natural highway of lakes and rivers used by the Voyageurs, the French traders and trappers who were among the very first to penetrate into and settle the interior of the country.

Today the railroads for the most part remain. The Canadian National has become privatized, and although Anne of Green Gables may continue to ride the rails as she does in Lucy Maude Montgomery's celebrated literary classic set in Prince Edward Island, that province has only a few old stations, pillars of abandoned trestles, and a museum to remind itself that once the trains ran here. Newfoundland's narrow-gauge line was undoubtedly doomed if for no other reason than the idiosyncrasy of its track. Nevertheless, much remains as it always has. With a certain amount of determination you can still ride as a passenger all the way between Vancouver and Halifax, even if no longer on a single train. Should you have a mind to visit the polar bears of Churchill in northern Manitoba, Via Rail's *Hudson Bay* can take you there. If you are fortunate you may get some memorable views of the Northern Lights as a bonus as you ride across the tundra.

The trains continue to run, but they no longer can link the nation as they once did. If Canadian trade once was mostly an East-West affair, today it is more likely North-South. Most of Alberta's oil and natural gas go to the United States. The same is true of Ontario's automobile parts and Quebec's hydroelectric power. Much of the prairie's wheat travels to Vancouver to ultimately leave the country headed for Pacific Rim ports. If Canada is to remain as one, it must discover new forces with the power to attract diverse people and places, forces with the sensitivity to protect rather than smother that diversity but with the power to create a unity where the natural one is indeed sometimes fragile.

THE GRAND TOUR

Hopefully by now some of the diversity and complexity that is Canada has begun to emerge. This country is truly a mosaic, each piece contributing to the complex whole. It is time to more closely examine some of those parts to discover the wonders each has to contribute.

Newfoundland and Labrador

An artist's interpretation of a Newfoundland postage stamp has added to the original portrait of some fish the motto "In Cod we Trust." Although it may no longer be the case, for centuries this was certainly true. It is probable that even before the voyages of Columbus made the "discovery" of the New World official for Europeans, adventuresome fishermen risked their lives to fish the rich Grand Banks off the Newfoundland coast. Salt cod, which could be shipped almost anywhere in the world, ultimately made this Britain's wealthiest colony, and Water Street in downtown St. John's, the provincial capital, proudly proclaimed itself North America's oldest avenue.

So rich was the island that for a time Britain would discourage settlement here, fearful that some other power might seize control. It was illegal to build a residence with a chimney, and of course without a chimney one could not survive the fierce Newfoundland winters.

Ultimately the "no settlements" policy was a failure, and the island became the sight of some of the oldest communities on this side of the Atlantic. In fact Trinity claims to be the oldest in North America, even if its beginnings might be considered more or less "unofficial." Eventually Britain would have to battle the French for control of this rich prize, but at last she was successful, although in a way Paris would have the final word. It still controls St. Pierre et Miquelon, two small islands and their surrounding waters, off the southwest coast of Newfoundland.

In addition to the wealth of the seas, Newfoundland yielded timber for the ships of the British Navy, and lumber and paper pulp remain island enterprises to the present. Representatives from Newfoundland did attend the 1864 discussions at Charlottetown, Prince Edward Island, which led to the establishment of the Canadian Confederation three years later, but in the end the colony declined to join. With the wealth of the Grand Banks it saw little commercial advantage to the proposed union, and given its rather isolated location, well to the east, unlike the other provinces, it had little fear of any sort of American invasion. By 1855 the island had achieved responsible government, which meant its residents had nearly complete control over their domestic political affairs, without interference from London. The result of all of this was a proud, hard-working, independent people, strongly loyal to the mother country, and with only modest interest in their Canadian neighbor.

Technology benefits most people, but the price for this is the nasty tricks it plays on others. Refrigeration destroyed much of the market for salt cod, and sails gave way to steam power. In addition the fishery gradually became exhausted by the combination of two many fishermen and too efficient harvesting methods. Today some lament that Newfoundland's major export seems to be its educated young people, who have the opportunity to go elsewhere in search of a better and easier life. As early as the years of the Great Depression the colony was on the verge of economic collapse and had to ask London to replace responsible government with a commission under British control to try to put its fiscal house back in order. In 1949, largely for the financial benefits they would receive, the islanders joined Canada as the tenth province. Much of the credit for persuading them to take this reluctant step must go to

Newfoundland's native son Joey Smallwood, who is often called the last Father of Confederation. Smallwood, who became the first provincial premier and undertook bold steps to revitalize and diversify the economy, understood Newfoundland's future lay with Canada. Often controversial, on this point at least, today he is seen as mostly right.

Joey Smallwood also understood the riches of the "Land of Cain," the vast, often inhospitable mainland portion of the province that lies to the north of the island of Newfoundland. (In 2001 the federal government officially renamed Newfoundland as Newfoundland and Labrador, the designation already widely used at the provincial level.) As I stood on the deck of the first ferry from Newfoundland to briefly stop at the coastal community of Cartwright, during the short summer season, before going further north to Goose Bay, I began to better understand how remote most of Labrador is. Almost everybody in town seemed to be gathering at the dock to catch a glimpse of this rare intrusion from the rest of the world. Time for a brief stroll enabled me to come across a long-abandoned Hudson's Bay Company outpost slowly and quietly disintegrating in the harsh Northern winters. Only later did I learn that it was here, while an employee of the company, that Henry Birdseye developed the process for frozen food. Perhaps this was how he kept his mind active in the winter darkness. Undoubtedly Birdseye would have appreciated the southern branch of the Trans-Labrador Highway that since 2003 has linked Cartwright with communities to the south and will eventually extend further north and west to Goose Bay.

However, Smallwood understood that if Labrador is a land that can be inhospitable, it is also one that can reluctantly yield wealth to those with the courage to challenge her. With Quebec he developed the hydroelectric potential of the Churchill (Grand) River at Churchill Falls, but at the price of giving most of the profits away to his French-speaking neighbors. Perhaps they see that as only fair, since they feel their legal claim to this land is really as valid as that of Newfoundland. In the interior, rich iron deposits are exploited at Wabush and Labrador City, while the dual community of Happy Valley-Goose Bay remains primarily a military outpost, for NATO.

Further north in Labrador at Voisey's Bay the Inco Corporation has constructed a huge nickel complex, although there were complications. In the spirit of Smallwood, Brian Tobin, the former Newfoundland premier who went on to serve in the federal government, called for Inco to not only mine at Voisey's Bay but to build a smelter on the island of Newfoundland which would create several thousand badly-needed jobs as well as refine the ore. For economic reasons Inco preferred to build its smelter elsewhere. Fortunately in June 2002 Inco and the province reached an agreement. The island will get a smelter and the resulting jobs by 2011. In the meantime Inco will have the right to ship the ore it began mining in September 2005 to its present smelters in Sudbury, Ontario, and Thompson, Manitoba.

Some folks in Labrador feel that such island concerns have often been put first and theirs second. Probably most understand the province usually has the highest unemployment rate in the country, but they may also feel that too many islanders come up to take jobs in Labrador that should go to those who already live there. Some, such as members of the United Labrador Movement, feel so strongly about it that they fly their own flag and advocate secession, not from Canada, but from the province of Newfoundland.

Hopefully the province will stay intact. Ottawa realizes in the future the fishery can never supply enough jobs. Leaders such as Tobin, and those who have come afterward, know diversification is the solution. I had breakfast one morning in St. John's with a Korean businessman. He was interested in seafood, but not codfish. Sea urchins and other marine life that may be considered useless or a nuisance by North Americans turn up on the tables of Asian families. He could see all sorts of possibilities. Many Canadians see exporting Newfoundland and Labrador's fresh water to the thirsty United States as an environmental threat, and currently it is not legal. Some Newfoundlanders feel this is another future industry. One small company already bottles iceberg water, which is sold locally. The rich Hibernia oilfield off the coast did not bring the vast number of jobs some expected, but it has helped breathe some new economic life into the province. Newfoundlanders are survivors. They have to be to live on this granite rock of an island that refuses to give to the faint-hearted. Somehow I think they will manage, and their numbers will include those who actually thrive. I met one woman who not only operated a bed and breakfast, but, along with a business partner, started a travel agency. She was not asking for an opportunity. She made her own. She is not alone.

The Maritimes

The Maritimes gave birth to the Canadian nation. Wander the halls of Province House in Charlottetown, Prince Edward Island, and you begin to feel that you will come across the Fathers of Confederation hammering out the agreement for the creation of the new country. The host colony, Prince Edward Island, would wait a few years, until 1871, to join, because of complications over land titles, but New Brunswick and Nova Scotia signed on along with Ontario and Quebec, and in 1867 the British North America Act made the union official. Despite the hopes of increased trade and better defense against a feared American invasion, there was reluctance to give up the independence of going it alone, but in the end they did, and the nation was born.

Prince Edward Island:

The three Maritime Provinces are Canada's smallest ones. Prince Edward Island, is the smallest of the three but among the most peaceful of all ten. Today it stands at a crossroad, as since 1997 it has been linked for the first time to the rest of Canada by a great bridge that connects it with New Brunswick. Until then its isolation and tranquility were protected, as they could only be breached by ferry or air. Unfortunately isolation not only protects tranquility but can also retard economic development, and ultimately the Islanders felt they best risk the causeway. However, much of the serenity of the place remains, and it has the power to take one back to what seems to be a calmer, gentler time. On Prince

Edward Island you can still find an absence of skyscraper office buildings and gentle farms that extend all the way to the sea. Here the waters of the Gulf of St. Lawrence are warm enough that salt-water swimming is actually enticing during the Canadian summer. Things will undoubtedly change. In time there will be more condominiums, more golf courses, higher land prices, more traffic congestion, and all the rest of the things that go with development. Much of the island's innocence will be lost forever, but more of its young people will be able to stay home rather than go off to universities elsewhere and then employment in Toronto, Montreal, or Vancouver. Enough of the potato farmers, lobstermen, and the modest homes with their French Acadian flags proudly flying in the yard will remain to remind those who care enough to be reminded what the soul of Prince Edward Island actually is.

Nova Scotia:

Nova Scotia was the original home of most of those Acadians. Henry Wadsworth Longfellow's *Evangeline* is a fictional character, but the heroic Acadian woman has left her name upon this land, the Land of Evangeline. The Acadians were among the first European settlers in North American. Hardworking French farmers, they asked nothing more than to stay out of the conflict between France and Britain for control of this part of the world. That was not to be. Some managed to flee to Prince Edward Island or hide in the interior of New Brunswick, but in 1755 most were expelled by the British who were suspicious of their professed neutrality. The two nations would continue to struggle for control of the area, with England holding on to Halifax and the French controlling Cape Breton Island from their still-standing fortress at Louisburg. Eventually Britain would win out, and ultimately Nova Scotia would become a refuge for American Loyalists who wanted nothing to do with a revolution against King George III. Among their numbers were some of the earliest African Americans to settle in Canada. Many would eventually move on to Sierra Leone, the colony established in West Africa for freed slaves, but others would remain. Their descendants are among the citizens of Canada today.

Perhaps the most intriguing of all Nova Scotians were those alleged to have arrived before the official dawn of European discovery. Legends persist of a Scottish nobleman, Henry Sinclair, having made a voyage to Nova Scotia in 1398 and successfully founding a colony there. Some believe that Sinclair's colonists may have had some involvement with the mysterious Money Pit on Oak Island, said to hold an undisclosed treasure, which still eludes recovery to the present day. Possibly in some way Sinclair's colonists were later linked to the founding of Montreal in Quebec, but at this point the story of the exploits of Henry Sinclair must remain speculation, even if a most fascinating one.

In certain ways the early economic history of Nova Scotia seems to parallel that of Newfoundland. Actually this is true of all of the Maritime Provinces. Fishing and forest resources provided a challenging but good living for the early settlers. For Nova Scotia, Cape Breton Island once yielded a good deal of coal, and the province even hosted some commercial gold mining as well as the expected agriculture. In the twentieth century government payrolls were very important to its economic life, as it was, among other things, a vital area for the Canadian military.

Today the situation is changing. Nova Scotia, especially Cape Breton, has known more than its share of economic difficulty. Even the relatively brief drive tourists take from the historic Citadel in downtown Halifax to picturesque Peggy's Cove, with its much-photographed lighthouse and post office, reveals in places a landscape harsh and unyielding. The entire Maritime region has seen traditional industries decline and unemployment rise, yet the populace has fought back and seems to be successfully meeting the challenge. Declining government employment has to some extent been replaced by companies specializing in data processing, which undoubtedly benefit from the area's well-deserved reputation for outstanding university education. The tourists are encouraged to come to Peggy's Cove, drive Cape Breton's majestic Cabot Trail, and discover the moving history of this land. An increasing number of Americans, along with Canadians from elsewhere in the country, have liked what they have seen so much that they have touched off something of a real estate boom, especially in the coastal areas. Sable Island, which lies about150 miles east of the coast and was once known primarily as a graveyard for North American shipping, is now acquiring a reputation as a rich area for natural gas and petroleum. Clearly those with courage and vision may find that Nova Scotia has a strong magnetic attraction.

New Brunswick:

As I noted earlier, on a rather cool and cloudy October morning, while walking along the banks of the St. John River in the New Brunswick capital of Fredericton, in a seemingly forgotten gathering surrounded by low bushes, I came across a few crumbling stones. They were all that was left of the markers in the original Loyalist cemetery. Somehow they had the ability to transport back in time, and one could sense how tragic that original winter must have been for these who were among the very first to flee the rebellious colonies further south because they wanted to remain faithful to their mother country. Many did not survive that first winter. Others perished in the winters to follow and are buried, along with the soldiers ultimately sent to protect them, in a more visible cemetery in the center of town.

The city's old Anglican cathedral, with its stain-glass windows made from a forgotten process utilizing gold, looks as if it could have been directly transported from England. It serves as yet another reminder of the colonists' roots. As provincial capitals go, Fredericton is not a large one, but its streets retain something of the charm of earlier days. One can watch with admiration and amazement as pewter smiths cast artifacts of beauty on what looks much like a potter's wheel.

Although Loyalists were among the first European settlers in the province, they were not the only ones. Acadians found it attractive, and of course even earlier the Micmacs and other Indian bands, as tribes are called in Canada, immigrated into the area. Today New Brunswick is the only province outside Quebec where a considerable amount of the population, over 30 percent, claim French as the language of the home, and New Brunswick is the only province in the country that is officially bilingual. While Canada is bilingual at the federal level of government, at the provincial level, outside of New Brunswick, English is the official language, with Quebec of course designating French. Essential services are provided in both languages throughout the entire country. New Brunswick thus serves as a unique reminder of the dual origins of the Canadian nation.

The province has also played a part in American history. As a boy Franklin Roosevelt spent his summers at the family retreat on Campobello Island. The living room of the home looks over Friar's Bay. One cannot help but wonder if while viewing and exploring the waters around Campobello, if the young Roosevelt first heard tales about Oak Island and its treasure. He would later take part in one unsuccessful attempt to recover it. The Roosevelt home is preserved in the Roosevelt Campobello International Park and is administered by the United States and Canada through the Roosevelt Campobello International Park Commission, the only jointly administered area in the entire American National Park system. It is easily reached by bridge from the town of Lubec, Maine.

Today New Brunswick faces an economic situation somewhat similar to the rest of Atlantic Canada. Diversification is strongly needed, since timber and the sea can no longer provide the strength to the economy they once did. Tourism has further potential with such attractions as the mysterious tidal bore of the Bay of Fundy, and the fascinating Reversing Falls the tide creates at Saint John, along with the scenic coasts, but other industries are also necessary. The residents seem to be aware of this and the advantage of close, working-relationships with areas outside the province. It was a former premier who took the lead in starting the effort that ultimately led to the Calgary Accord, an effort to try to reach some common ground between Quebec and the other nine provinces. In a Fredericton taxi I was surprised to have the driver ask me what people in my town thought about the new Free Trade Agreement (pre-NAFTA) between the United States and Canada. I could not bring myself to respond that they probably had not thought about it at all. It was obvious from his remarks that like others in the province he hoped it would bring prosperity and a better future. All of the Maritimes still have economic hurdles to clear, but give them credit for working hard at it.

Quebec

It was on the Plains of Abraham, at the edge of Quebec City, that I think for the first time I was able to penetrate the soul of the francophone citizens of this province. Certainly Quebecers wish to protect their language, religion, and culture. More so, they wish to protect their dignity. It was here that General Wolfe's forces defeated those of General Montcalm, both leaders dying in the battle, but in this decisive struggle of the Seven Years War New France was destroyed, and the British North American Empire grew dramatically.

At first perhaps the residents of New France did not think this was such a catastrophe. They had been here a long time, ever since Samuel de Champlain had established Quebec City in 1608. Further up the St. Lawrence River Montreal could trace its origins back to 1642. This land seemed almost as French as France itself. Surely they expected that they would be traded for territory France had gained elsewhere and that Britain wanted. Such trades were a commonly accepted practice after the wars of that day. In time Britain and France would arrange a trade, but the French chose the sugar-rich Caribbean islands of Martinique and Guadeloupe instead. The *habitants* of New France had been abandoned for good.

British rule was actually rather benign. Perhaps thinking they would not control the territory long anyway, London had granted the Quebec Act in 1773, which protected the territory's language, religion, and judicial system. The grateful populace would remain loyal during the American Revolution, although the rebels would attack Quebec City and for a time even hold part of Montreal. Still British administrators were not French ones. No longer able to obtain guidance from the leadership of their original homeland, Quebecers turned to the only institution left that they felt was truly theirs, the Roman Catholic Church. The church helped them preserve their identity and made a deep impression on their culture, one that remains to the present day. However, its defensive approach was one that encouraged an inward rather than outward posture. Tend to your farms, raise your children, practice your religion, obey the law, and avoid unnecessary contact with the authorities. As a result, the *habitants*, as the French population was known, survived and even felt secure, but they paid a price. Economic and, to some extent, political control of the province gradually fell into the hands of Canadians of English ancestry. In the later part of the nineteenth century nearly half the population of Quebec City was English-speaking. In World Wars I and II, Quebecers, who certainly had no love of European dictatorships or fascism, bitterly resented conscription, since they felt that their sons were expected to die for a foreign policy crafted in London and followed by a knee-jerk reaction in Ottawa. Symbolic of this is perhaps the sending of the Quebec Rifles to assist in the token defense of Hong Kong, which inevitably fell to the Japanese.

The Quiet Revolution of the 1960s began to change things. The church's influence would gradually diminish. Young francophones would begin to take control of the provincial economy, at the price of some businesses fleeing Montreal to establish their headquarters in Toronto, or elsewhere in Canada. Politically sovereignists, with their demands for independence began to grow in number while federalists, desiring to remain part of Canada, called for a new relationship, more protective of the Quebec people as a nation.

Often forgotten in this family argument between French and English speakers is the fact that few, if any, sovereignists have ever called for a total break with Canada. Rene Levesque, former provincial premier, and one of the founders of the separatist Parti Quebecois coined the term sovereignty-association. While it means different things to different people, elements often included are a relationship between Canada and Quebec which would permit a common currency and passport, customs union, freedom of passage, and possibly a single citizenship and freedom of immigration. Some have even advocated a consultative parliament and a common defense. English Canada may declare it looks as if Quebecers want to have their cake and eat it too, but if nothing else there is a certain irony here that sovereignty-association actually reveals a closer and different type of relationship between Quebec and the rest of Canada than many on both sides of the argument may care to admit. Perhaps francophones who feel fully in command and control of their identity and destiny could remain comfortably in Canada. The challenge is to find an acceptable way to do that.

Regardless of what the ultimate political future of Quebec may be, its economic future appears to be positive. Wandering along a thoroughfare in Prague, capital of the Czech Republic, I was somewhat surprised to come across the Quebec Trade Office, which was promoting economic activity with this promising central European nation. There has been a Quebec trade official stationed in Orlando, Florida, at times when the federal government had no similar representative there. Certainly the province is serious about promoting commerce. It aggressively advertises tourism to an increasingly interested American market, skillfully marketing both summer and winter activities. Clearly here it has a lot to offer with northern wilderness, fishing, skiing, winter carnival, and in Quebec City, with its celebrated Hotel Chateau Frontenac, the only walled city in North America north of Mexico. The shrine of Ste. Anne de Beaupre, a short distance northeast of Quebec City, is one of the continent's most popular destinations for religious pilgrimages.

Politically the Parti Quebecois may advocate sovereignty and the protection of the French language, but it also promotes more English study in the schools, recognizing its value for business purposes. This is one place where separatist and federalist agree. I have even heard a minister in a former Parti Quebecois provincial government proudly proclaim how many trilingual people were now to be found in the Montreal area. All Quebec political leaders are strong supporters of NAFTA (North American Free Trade Agreement) and thus recognize the value of fluency in Spanish as well as French and English.

Quebec's trade with the United States may trail that of neighboring Ontario, but it is growing and is less than that of only a small handful of nations. Quebec Hydro is vital to meeting the energy needs of New York State and other Northeastern areas of the United States. The St. Lawrence Seaway is indispensable to both American and Canadian commerce. In still other ways the province's businesses demonstrates their value. Its aluminum, paper and pulp, and pharmaceutical industries are significant. The Montreal Stock Exchange, the nation's oldest, in cooperation with the other stock exchanges, handles nearly all the derivatives business in the country as well as listing Quebec junior companies. Montreal-based Bombardier dominates the market for mass-transit equipment while also providing competition for both Boeing and Airbus. Clearly the question of separation should not be permitted to so obscure the view that the rest of what is happening in Quebec is missed.

Ontario

In a very real sense there are actually two provinces that comprise Ontario. The first is the Lower Peninsula, the part of Canada most heavily populated and best known to Americans. The second is the rest of the province, which stretches from the shores of Lakes Superior and Huron all the way north to Hudson Bay. There is quite a contrast between the two. The upwelling of the Laurentian Shield, a granite range of hills and small mountains that extends across Quebec and Ontario, is responsible for this second land. Covered with lakes and forests, but with little topsoil, it is not a hospitable area for agriculture. Few large cities are found here, although, thanks to the Great Lakes and the St. Lawrence Seaway, Thunder Bay, on the north shore of Lake Superior, is Canada's major grain port, moving large quantities of prairie wheat and other grains to Europe and additional destinations. The region is supportive of lumbering and mining, and the low but steep slopes even provide good winter skiing, but outside a few communities such as Sault Ste. Marie and Timmins the population is modest and likely to remain that way, at least in the near future. There is some relatively quiet concern here that the Lower Peninsula is apt to take this more northern area for granted, forgetting sometimes it even exists. That would be a mistake, for certainly there is potential here, but it is overshadowed by Canada's business heartland, the Lower Peninsula of Ontario. Stretching from Windsor, across the Detroit River from Detroit, Michigan, through London and on to Hamilton, Toronto, Oshawa, Kingston, and Ottawa, this is a dynamic land that seems to reject limits or boundaries to its future.

Striking evidence of the economic power of the area is the seldom-realized fact that Ontario is the second largest trading partner of the United States. Only Canada as a whole does more business with America than this single province. Southern Ontario (along with Montreal) has always been the national Canadian economic heartland. Today it seems on the verge of becoming something even more. Thomas Courchene and Colin Telmer, of the University of Toronto's Centre for Public Management now see it as a "North American region state," possibly the preeminent one. As it continues to take more control of its political and economic situation from Ottawa, Ontario will be in a position "to pursue its own destiny, on its own terms." That does not have to be bad for the rest of Canada or for North America, but it should yield tremendous benefits for the progress of the province as it enters a yet-to-be-fully-determined future. Regardless of the final outcome, Ontario stands to greatly benefit from free trade, more provincial power, and further economic expansion.

A careful walk around southern Ontario's major cities or even a train ride along the shore of Lake Ontario can be quite revealing. Oshawa is sometimes called "Canada's Detroit." General Motors has its impressive headquarters here. If you look at the panel of the front door of your "American" General Motors car it just may read: "Made in Oshawa." This is the national economic heartland, but it is much more. Here is where today's multicultural Canada can remember its roots. Southern Ontario is United Empire Loyalists country, populated with communities quite proud of their heritage and ready to proclaim it. Their founders settled here not seeking revolution or independence but rather loyalty to the monarch, order, and good government. In this part of the nation, many would see the Queen's portrait on currency and other traditional symbols that link Canada with Britain as highly appropriate and hardly outdated.

Elements of the past persist and remain significant. Maybe outside of Canada it would be impossible for them to coexist with something newer and far more complex, but here they manage to do so. Maybe Toronto, Ontario's provincial capital, and today the nation's largest city and commercial capital, is the most vibrant symbol of all of this. You can visit the city's original settlement, Fort York, downtown near the lakefront. A large Hudson's Bay Company department store does business here, and maybe in some ways the Sky Dome is a sign of American influence since it is the home of baseball's American-League Toronto Blue Jays. Yet look around you. There is a lot more. Perhaps the city's restaurants are an even more important symbol. Toronto appears to have an endless supply of every sort of ethnic food imaginable. This is not the result of coincidence but rather that of immigration. Over one-third of the city's population is classified as "visible minorities," people who not only look different but who have brought their cultural traditions with them.

Metropolitan Toronto is filled with ethnic neighborhoods, specialty stores, schools where children are comfortable learning in a language that is not their mother tongue, and other signs that dynamic change has occurred. It would be foolish to think that such a mix of peoples brings with it only complete harmony and never any tension. Nevertheless, Toronto and other places in Canada have made multiculturalism work. In the global economy of today it is difficult to imagine a better economic advantage. Look out, world. Here comes Ontario.

The Prairies

The Laurentian Shield eventually gives way to the rich soils of the Canadian prairies and the country's traditional agricultural heartland. This area is also changing, and the distinctive Canadian-style grain elevator that served as a proud monument in almost every prairie community is rapidly fading away to be replaced by a larger, more efficient facility or by nothing at all. In many cases farms have been consolidated, and to a considerable extent industry and services have challenged agriculture for its place in the economy. Certainly this part of the country is evolving, and the process is far from finished. It has always been a place of opportunity for those with the necessary courage and vision. Despite certain difficulties, that should be the case in the future as well.

Manitoba

The most impressive hotel in Winnipeg, capital of Manitoba, is the Hotel Louis Riel. Not only is it a pleasant place to stay, but its name serves as a reminder of the enigma that one sometimes encounters even in the modern Manitoba. In this, the most eastern of the Prairie Provinces, you will find Riel's grave in the cemetery of St. Boniface Cathedral. At one time St. Boniface with its French and Metis population was a separate city, but now it is a part of Winnipeg. Services in the cathedral are in French; however, you will find that nearly everyone in St. Boniface also speaks English, although this is the largest francophone community in Western Canada.

Settlement of the prairies was born at Winnipeg, and both the Metis and Riel are part of that story. The place where the Assinibone and Red River come together, The Forks, as it is now commonly called, was the site of one of the earliest efforts to claim the prairies. While there already were some French and British immigrants in the area, in 1821 the Hudson's Bay Company established the Red River settlement, with most of the settlers being either Voyageurs, who were French trappers and traders, or Metis, the offspring of Voyageur marriages to Indian brides. That same year the Company absorbed its rival, the North West Company, which had tried unsuccessfully to destroy the earlier British settlements in a failed effort for control of the lucrative fur trade. In a small park in downtown Winnipeg, across the street from the Fort Garry Hotel, stands the gate of Upper Fort Garry, the focal point of Hudson's Bay's vital Red River outpost. The rest of the fort has long disappeared, but Lower Fort Garry, a modest distance north of Winnipeg, still remains intact and enables visitors to better comprehend life on the prairie frontier.

Louis Riel, was born in 1844 in Red River and eventually returned after being educated in Montreal and working for a time in St. Paul, Minnesota. In 1869 he would emerge as the Metis leader. He proved successful in his struggle to bring Manitoba into the Canadian Confederation in 1870 as the country's fifth province (even before Prince Edward Island) while winning rights for the French-speaking settlers and Metis. Difficulties with the federal government ultimately forced him to immigrate to Montana and become an American citizen, only to return to Canada to organize the desperate Indians and Metis who were in dire economic condition and felt that they were being neglected by the government while at the same time losing their land. At Batouche, in neighboring

Saskatchewan, Riel's forces went down to a final defeat, and he was captured. Found guilty of treason, he was hanged in 1885, despite pleas to Prime Minister John Macdonald to spare his life. A man of sincere, deep religious faith, Riel appears to have died with dignity, courage, and with no malice toward the government. After his death his body lay in state for two days at the still-standing St. Boniface home of his mother before final burial. His execution left a wound that has not entirely healed to the present day.

The execution of Louis Riel undoubtedly did much to strain relationships between English and French-speaking Canada. He remains controversial even now. While still traitor for some, he is hero to many more, and it was decided to honor him with a statue. However, it had to be placed just beyond the grounds of Winnipeg's legislative building, since technically Riel has never been pardoned. So the memorial to the province's founder has a place of prominence and honor, but perhaps not quite on the spot where most think it should be. Also adding to the irony is the fact that this, a rather traditional portrayal of the rather handsome Riel, is actually the second statue. The first, a more modern, impressionistic work, was rejected by much of Winnipeg's Metis population, particularly the older members, who viewed it as a twisted distortion. It was removed to the grounds of a school, some of whose students seem to sense it tries to interpret the struggle and pain that were indeed part of the life of this Canadian hero.

Others were destined to play a happier role in the early settlement of the Manitoba prairies. The celebrated Red River ox carts would bring the first pioneers in search of fertile, productive land. They would eventually give way to the railroad and the arrival of immigrants enticed by rail and steamship advertisements along with government promises of cheap land. They came from various parts of Central and Eastern Europe and on into Russia and the Ukraine. The prairie soils always served as a magnet, but for some, such as the Hutterites, religious freedom and the opportunity to preserve a unique way of life were just as important.

Many of the settlers prospered. It is quite logical that Canada's grain exchanges are located in Winnipeg. Wheat continues to play an important part in the provincial economy, but today it is only part of the story.

Service industries, such as finance and insurance, are major players as well. Petroleum production, along with manufacturing, adds to the mix, and Winnipeg remains a transportation hub. The world-acclaimed Winnipeg Ballet Company, with its impressive headquarters in the city, is an appropriate symbol of the dynamic life to be found here.

Perhaps surprisingly, most of Manitoba is not prairie land at all. It consists of lakes, dominated by gigantic Lake Winnipeg, and forests. Northern Manitoba yields timber, hydroelectric power, and mineral wealth, with Inco operating a major nickel mine in the interior at Thompson. By rail it ends at the "Polar Bear Capital of the World," Churchill on the west shore of Hudson Bay, and in the ice-free season from mid-July to early November the shortest route for grain shipments to Europe is from the port of Churchill.

Saskatchewan

In a way my introduction to Saskatchewan was actually in Churchill. While searching for baluga whales one August, along with hopes of spotting an early polar bear, I made the journey to this intriguing sub-Arctic town that even most Canadians have never visited. I found both whale and bear, which were well worth the visit, but quite unexpectedly had the opportunity to strike up some brief friendships with wheat farmers from Saskatchewan who had been invited to town by the Hudson Bay Route Association. Annually this organization encourages farmers from Saskatchewan and Manitoba to make the trip to Churchill in the hope that they will then decide to export at least some of their grain through the port. The Association claims just 4 percent of the European wheat exports is enough to make the port profitable, but it must fiercely compete with Thunder Bay for even that. Some of these farmers came from the community with the distinctive name of Hudson Bay (not to be confused with the body of water), Saskatchewan, and other towns near there, but most seemed to have arrived from the area around Canora, Saskatchewan. They were a friendly bunch and most impressive. Although I had flown into Churchill on a white-knuckle flight during an

August storm, which at the time seemed more appropriate for January, I had the opportunity and the relief to ride as far as Canora with my new friends on the train taking me back to Winnipeg.

Obviously farming was not what it once had been. It still took plenty of work and a willingness to gamble somewhat on nature and world grain prices, but it was now accomplished with the aid of computers and access to futures prices on the commodity exchanges. Efficient utilization of modern and expensive machinery required small farms to be merged into larger ones. Clearly successful farmers had to be very intelligent farmers with the ability to plan effectively. Most of these folks, although worried about the possibility of frost earlier than usual in September, seemed pretty accomplished at it. Some were not happy about having to sell their wheat and barley through the government-sponsored Wheat Board, which producers of most other agricultural commodities and Eastern farmers were not required to do, but over the years they had managed to live with this situation as well. I had to admit I was very impressed. If it were possible to prosper in agriculture these folks surely would. Although things have since improved considerably, in past years there was a drop in wheat and other grain prices, one that began when Asian currencies suffered from the "Asian flu" in October of 1997. Grain exports to the Pacific Rim underwent major declines. Worldwide prices headed South. More recently there was also drought with which to contend. Difficult times came to the prairies, even for the best of farmers. However, this was not the first time.

As a result of the plight of prairie farmers and workers during the Great Depression, the Co-operative Commonwealth Federation was born in Calgary in 1932, the creation of labor leaders, farmers, and intellectuals. Under the leadership of Methodist minister James Shaver Woodsworth, the new party was an unusual blend of religious fundamentalism and socialism, issuing the rather radical Regina Manifesto of 1933, calling for government social and economic planning. However, it was a Baptist minister, Tommy Douglas, who led the CCF to victory in an innovative but more moderate direction. In 1944 Douglas and the CCF were voted into power in Saskatchewan. As Premier, Douglas fully understood the plight of the farmers and their families that began during the Depression and continued through World War II. When the going gets tough the tough get creative. Under Douglas the CCF tried new solutions to improve the economic situation and the welfare of the populace. Some might even be called a kind of non-Marxist socialism. Several of these worked, but by far the most impressive was a provincial-government sponsored free hospitalization plan, the first in the nation. Building on the work of Douglas, in 1962 the CCF, now renamed the New Democratic Party, under Premier Woodrow Lloyd, introduced medicare in Saskatchewan. It became the model for the provincially administered, federally and provincially funded, national health system operating today in all the provinces and territories. It is not perfect, but most Canadians are proud of it and point to it as one of the major factors that makes Canada a caring nation and a good place to live. They may feel that today it needs improvement, but few would call for its abolishment. The NDP has dropped any calls for socialism, but all political parties support government-sponsored health care. Saskatchewan farmers are tough and innovative. They always survive, and eventually many will once again thrive.

Today the provincial economy, like that of Manitoba, shows healthy signs of diversification. In addition to agriculture, manufacturing is growing, and there is steel production as well. Potash mining is also an important industry. Potash Corporation of Saskatchewan is a very successful company with a listing on the New York Stock Exchange as well as Toronto. The capital city, Regina, and Saskatoon are centers for a variety of economic activity. Innovation is also cutting costs in the still-important agricultural sector of the province's economy. The country's oldest and largest grain cooperative, Saskatchewan Wheat Pool, has developed methods to make storing and shipping more efficient and less expensive. Saskatchewan should continue to play a key role in future world agricultural markets.

Alberta

Americans traveling in Canada may feel particularly comfortable in Alberta, especially in the southern areas of the province around Calgary. This might almost be expected, because Alberta has attracted a considerable number of American immigrants. Like Texas, Oklahoma, and several other American states, the economy is heavily based on oil and natural gas production. Much of this is sold to the United States, thus creating even closer ties. Calgary's "trademark" is the famous Stampede, which turns the entire city's attention toward what is undoubtedly the world's largest rodeo. It may be Canadian, but Americans will feel right at home.

Also adding to this feeling of affinity is the lure of the Canadian Rockies. Experience the grandeur of Banff and Jasper National Parks, and you will not soon forget them. The Banff Springs Hotel seems to be one of the most photographed establishments in the world, and with good reason. The views of and from the hotel are awe-inspiring. Banff's Lake Louise is another one of those places so serene that visitors always hope that someday they will be able to return.

Of course further to the north people in the provincial capital of Edmonton might claim that here is the real heart of Alberta. This is a sophisticated city, one of the few large ones in Canada that lies a considerable distance away from the border with the United States. Edmonton can also boast of one of the world's largest malls, the West Edmonton Mall, one so huge it can comfortably house an entire hotel, amusement park, and other attractions. Over six million people visit it annually.

Like Calgary, Edmonton is in the heart of Canada's major oil producing region, and like the other Prairie Provinces, the area early attracted immigrants from Eastern Europe. It is still quite proud of its Ukrainian heritage and recognizes it with a nearby cultural center. Of course it is not really surprising that immigration flourished in Alberta. The eastern part of the province is in the Canadian grain belt, along with Saskatchewan and Manitoba. In both Alberta and British Columbia climatic conditions suitable for crops extend much further north than they do in the rest of Canada, thus making this a land of hope and opportunity for those seeking a new start.

Alberta is one of Canada's wealthiest provinces. In addition to the petroleum industry, it is also the home of some major Canadian corporations including the Calgary-based Canadian Pacific Railway.

Calgary is also the location for one of the two branches of Canada's TSX Venture Stock Exchange, the other being in Vancouver. The TSX Venture Exchange lists the vast majority of Canadian small capitalization companies that are traded on an exchange in the country.

Success has not come without some problems. Many residents of Alberta, along with others from British Columbia, and to a certain extent the other Prairie Provinces, feel that Eastern Canada sometimes takes them for granted and at others tries to use them. During the 1973 oil crisis Prime Minister Pierre Trudeau unsuccessfully attempted to make Alberta's oil a national rather than a provincial resource. The response from the province was, "Let the Eastern bastards freeze in the dark." Albertans saw the federal government's actions as an illegal attempt to seize what was theirs.

They also believe they pay more than their share of the federal government's revenue while being underrepresented in the government. Residents are not without reasons. Alberta and Ontario send revenue to the federal government in Ottawa, which in turn makes equalization payments to the remaining provinces that have less wealth than these two leaders. The payments are essentially grants distributed to the provinces based on their population and standard of living, and may be used by the recipient governments as they see best. As their name indicates, their objective is to try to somewhat equalize the quality of life for all Canadians.

Even in the wealthier provinces there is some support for such programs as equalization payments. What disturbs the West is the fact that with its wealth and growing population it is under represented in the government. This is probably true more in the Canadian Senate than anywhere else. If the Senate had significant power, rather than the little it currently possesses, this would be an even more serious problem. Organizations such as the Canada West Foundation, with its headquarters in Calgary, do seek to bring the concerns that Alberta and the other Western provinces and territories have to the attention of the entire country. Probably the most critical point they seek to make is that Alberta and the rest of the West need to play a dynamic part in the shaping of Canada's future, no matter what that future may be. There can be little doubt that if this happens the entire country will be strengthened as a result. Maybe the election of a Conservative party government headed by Prime Minister Stephen Harper from Alberta in 2006 is a sign that the Canadian West will be more visible in the years to come.

British Columbia

Canada's most western province, British Columbia, is possibly more complex than even some Canadians may realize. The provincial capital, Victoria, near the southern end of Vancouver Island, is perhaps the most "British" of all Canadian cities. Sit down at high tea some afternoon at the venerable Empress Hotel overlooking the harbor, and you will capture just a touch of the life of the English gentry of earlier times. Double-decker sightseeing buses and other English touches add to the illusion.

Have breakfast in the hotel the next morning and you encounter another facet of British Columbia. In addition to the more typical offerings, you may dine on an Asian buffet. British Columbia makes Canada a Pacific Rim nation. Appropriately the mainland city of Vancouver, Canada's third largest, has a large Asian population.

Vancouver is typical of British Columbia's diversity. Truly multicultural, here you may also encounter a symbol of its earliest inhabitants, the Indian bands. Totem poles serve as reminders that people have long been attracted to the riches of the area. Off shore is a rich salmon fishery. Surrounding much of the city, forests come down from the spectacular mountains to meet up with the commercial center. Some 60 percent of Canada's commercial timber is harvested in British Columbia. The mineral wealth of the interior has been attracting settlers for a century and a half. Both Vancouver and the rest of the province have so much to offer in activities and some of the most spectacular scenery in North America that they have long been popular tourist destinations.

The beautiful but rugged and untamed landscape of this province has attracted and produced a distinct kind of people, often opportunistic and individualistic. They like to think for themselves and do things their way. Many share the concerns of their neighbors in Alberta that Ottawa does not always understand them and sometimes forgets them. However, there is little doubt they are destined to play a key role in Canada's tomorrow. In the 1980s and much of the 1990s they prospered more than any other part of Canada. Perhaps things got somewhat ahead of themselves, and the end of the last decade saw something of a slowdown. This certainly cannot last. The ingredients for success are still in place. Vancouver remains a vibrant communications and transportation center. It is ideally situated for trade with Asia, Australia, and the United States. Parts of the province enjoy a climate mild in comparison with the rest of Canada. These factors along with the beauty and wealth of the land should continue to provide economic growth and progress in the years to come.

The Territories

The political differences between Canada's three territories and ten provinces are no longer very great. At one time governed rather closely from Ottawa, the territories now handle most affairs for themselves. They do need a greater amount of financial assistance, and the Royal Canadian Mounted Police handle law enforcement within their boundaries, but they have their own elected legislatures with territorial administrations responsible to them. While technically they do not vote on Constitutional amendments, the Constitution calls for the country to consult with native peoples before making changes. Many of the residents of the territories are native peoples, either Indian bands or Inuit, as the Eskimos prefer to be called. Since we have taken a look at each of the provinces, let us complete our Grand Tour of Canada with a brief stop in the three territories, beginning with the most western.

Yukon Territory

In a way the story of the Yukon Territory actually begins in Seattle. In 1896 gold was discovered along the Klondike branch of the Yukon River. The fabled Klondike gold rush began the following year and would last a decade. Although few prospectors would find gold, and even fewer would manage to keep it, thousands would brave the hardships of the North for a chance at wealth. Most of these were Americans, and most would be outfitted and start the difficult journey north from Seattle. The National Park Service maintains a small but interesting museum in the city's Pioneer District that tells the prospectors' story. The lucky ones that survived the trek through White Pass or Chilkoot Pass often settled either around Dawson City or Whitehorse, the territorial capital. For a time these frontier towns enjoyed a rough kind of prosperity, but eventually most of the miners, if they were still alive, gave up and went home or moved on to the newer fields in Alaska.

Today someone traveling through the Yukon Territory most likely is on the highway leading to Alaska. It is a much easier journey now, although still not to be taken without proper preparations. The traveler will be rewarded with views of Canada's highest mountains, so high they are even unforgettable when spotted out of the window of an airplane. Some commercial mining activity continues in the Yukon along with a modest amount of tourism. Among its approximately 30,000 residents are a number of native peoples who manage to maintain elements of their traditional way of life.

The Northwest Territories

The Northwest Territories comprise a vast expanse of land, forest and tundra, punctuated with numerous lakes. Some of these, such as Great Slave Lake and Great Bear Lake are of very generous size. The area is sparsely populated but supports a variety of wildlife including an abundance of fish, moose, and caribou. Most of the aboriginal peoples here are Indian bands, particularly Dene, although there are a few Metis, and in the far north also some Inuit. Recent years have brought noticeable growth to the territorial capital of Yellowknife, which in addition to its somewhat primitive but fascinating historic district now can boast of downtown, modern, multistory buildings.

Hunting and fishing, both as a traditional way of life and as the basis for a tourist industry, are long established in the Northwest Territories. Some timber is also harvested, and oil is produced in the Norman Wells area of the Mackenzie Valley. Natural gas is found in the far north around Inuvik and close to Fort Laird, near the border with British Columbia. The Northwest Territories should benefit from future oil and gas pipelines.

Mining activities of various sorts, including copper, silver, uranium, and gold are also traditional economic activities that have been prosperous for many years. Yellowknife literally rests on top of old gold-mining shafts, and several mines still operate in the area, although the city's name is derived from copper deposits first worked by native peoples. A commercial fishery can be found at Hay River on the southern shore of Great Slave Lake

Perhaps most fascinating has been the relatively recent discovery of diamonds in the valley of the Mackenzie River and also in the territory north of Yellowknife. Several companies have now gone beyond the exploratory stage to actual commercial production. A successful diamond mine, costing over one billion Canadian dollars to develop, is operating north of Yellowknife.

The political future of the Northwest Territories remains cloudy. With fewer than 60,000 people it is too sparsely populated for provincial status. With a diverse population of both aboriginal and nonaboriginal peoples, it would not seem suitable to follow in the path of neighboring Nunavut, where the Inuit now have a homeland. Until the situation clarifies, and as the territorial infrastructure continues to develop and improve, modest population and economic growth seems to be a reasonable expectation.

Nunavut

On April 1, 1999, a major change was made in the map of Canada. In order to better understand what this means, it probably would be helpful to clarify a few things about the very first Canadians. When European explorers first set foot in what is now Canada they encountered people who had already been here for centuries. In the United States they are commonly known as American Indians or Native Americans. While the term Indian is used in Canada, they prefer to be known as First Nations. Native peoples and aboriginal peoples are also terms frequently used. What is known as an Indian tribe in the United States is referred to as an Indian band. Among the major bands today are the Dene and the Cree, while further south the Huron, Iroquois, and Mohawk are prevalent. The Huron may have been the largest group living in Canada when the first Europeans arrived.

First Nations are not the only group that qualifies as aboriginal peoples. The Metis have such status under the Canadian Constitution, as do the Inuit. It is the Inuit who are of particular interest when we turn to the birth of the territory known as Nunavut.

The term Inuit means "The People." It comes from the Inuktitut language that the Inuit speak. A single person would be referred to as an Inuk. Neither Inuit nor Inuk should be confused with the Innu, who are an Indian people, or First Nation, found in Labrador. Inuit understand that outsiders are not familiar with either their language or culture, so they will not take offense when they are called Eskimos. However, it is a term they really would prefer not to be used. Eskimo is a Cree Indian word meaning "eaters of raw flesh."

Perhaps this discussion over the usage and meaning of the term "Eskimo" reflects some of the tension between Inuit and other native peoples. Although things are somewhat more complex in the modern world, traditionally one did not find Indians dwelling in Inuit communities or Inuit on lands controlled by the various bands. The two groups have very different cultures, speak different languages, and sometimes had serious disputes over hunting and fishing rights. It is as wrong to see all aboriginal peoples as having the same interests and concerns as it would be to view all Europeans or Asians in such a matter.

Nunavut is an Inuktitut term meaning "Our Land." It is the land of the Inuit. Carved out of the Northwest Territories in 1999 as Canada's third territory, this is a huge expanse of land stretching from Hudson Bay all the way to Ellesmere Island, which parallels northern Greenland. The Inuit town of Grise Fiord, or Ausuituq in Inuktitut, on the southern shore of

Ellesmere Island, is Canada's most northern community. The severe climatic conditions require this to be a sparsely populated land. Only a little over 30,000 people call it home. Approximately 85 percent are Inuit.

The agreement between the government of Canada and the Inuit that gave birth to Nunavut sought to create a territory where the Inuit would be in charge of their own destiny and where their culture could thrive. In addition to monetary assistance, under the Inuit Land Claim they received an extensive amount of land and mineral rights in various parts of the territory and are guaranteed economic control as well. On the other hand, Nunavut definitely is no reservation or reserve. Anyone willing to brave the elements of the Arctic is welcome to live there. Several non-Inuit have been elected to the nonpartisan legislature that meets in the territorial capital of Iqaluit (formerly Frobisher Bay) on the southern end of Baffin Island.

No part of Canada faces more questions about its economic future than Nunavut. As dog sleds give way to snowmobiles (Skidoos, as they are commonly called in this part of the world), a traditional kind of life sometimes clashes with an imported culture. Hunting and fishing decline as a cash economy emerges. In some instances this has taken its toll on the male members of Inuit society, who may find their roles declining. Inuit women have been playing an increasingly stabilizing role in the region and its government. At one point Nunavut even gave serious consideration to gender parity for the legislature, but has tabled that idea at least for now. What is certain is that all the people of Nunavut are determined to seek solutions and create a stable and strong society that offers opportunity to future generations.

Indeed there are some positive signs. Nunavut tourism is increasing. The territory is rich in wildlife and the kind of beauty unique to Arctic regions. Remote Ellesmere Island National Park offers a wilderness experience almost impossible to find anyplace else. There are opportunities to learn and experience Inuit culture, and tour operators will take you all the way to the polar ice cap and the North Pole.

Artist and author James Houston deserves much of the credit for making the celebrated Inuit art known to the world. Today this creates a highly successful market and worldwide recognition for Inuit sculptors and print makers. Some galleries in the United States and Canada find the demand for these creations so great that they sell nothing but Inuit art. Those who have made purchases are not likely to be disappointed, as these items grow in both appreciation and monetary value.

Although the lack of infrastructure, a fragile environment, and the long, cold winters make conditions difficult, mining in the Arctic should increase. Commercial gold mining takes place, and Nunavut has additional mineral resources. The Inuit will undoubtedly seek to benefit from these in the future. Shrimp and scallop fishing also add to the economy.

There really is no other place like Nunavut. It is appropriate that our tour of Canada's provinces and territories ends here. Hopefully the unique blend of distinctive lands and peoples that comprise Canada has emerged. Canada is a land that cannot be duplicated. Now it is time to take a further look at how it was born and where it may be going.

A NATION IS BORN

A Brief Journey Through Canadian History

European Discovery

Although the Huron and Iroquois, along with other First Nations people were already here, legends abound as to when the first Europeans came across this land. One possibility is the Irish monk St. Brendan who some claim made a sixth-century Atlantic crossing, probably to Newfoundland, in a small hide-covered boat. Did the Scottish nobleman Henry Sinclair actually make a voyage to Nova Scotia in 1398? Were the Sinclairs in some way linked to the old Crusading order of the Knights Templars? Did they ultimately found a settlement and even help bury whatever it is that lies beneath mysterious Oak Island? There are tantalizing hints and theories, but we must await more solid evidence before reaching final conclusions. In the meantime you can find a monument to Sinclair's possible voyage in Boylston Park, Guysborough, Nova Scotia.

One thing is certain. The Vikings, or Norsemen, did reach Canada, most likely for the first time sometime between 860 and 1060. Archeological excavations between 1961 and 1967 at L'Anse-aux-Meadows, on the northern tip of Newfoundland, uncovered definite traces of a site at least briefly permanently inhabited by the Vikings.

Perhaps Leif Erikson may at sometime been one of the residents. Probably there were other Viking settlements in Canada. Viking artifacts have been found in numerous places in the Arctic regions of the country, including a trade-scale uncovered on remote Axel Helberg Island, west of Ellesmere Island. While it is impossible to say whether such items were carried by Viking explorers and traders or brought back by Inuit visiting Norse communities in Greenland, they serve as reminders that there is still much we do not fully know about the early history of this mysterious land.

The Italian Giovanni Caboto, better known to the world as John Cabot, in the service of England, is credited with the first visit to Canada during the European Age of Exploration. Exactly where he landed is the subject of much dispute, but Bonavista on Newfoundland is the traditional site, although it could have been almost anywhere between Labrador and Massachusetts. In any case, this 1497 discovery was a key element in the English claim to Newfoundland and its rich fishery on the Grand Banks. It is unlikely Cabot really was the first. Basque fishermen may have been fishing these waters as early as the fourteenth century but keeping that a secret in order to avoid competition.

French interest begins with the voyages of Jacques Cartier in 1534, 1535, and 1541, ultimately sailing up the St. Lawrence River as far as the site of Montreal. Cartier deserves credit for the naming of Canada. In 1535 two young Indians told him how to reach the settlement of Stradconna, on the site of Quebec City. They employed the Huron-Iroquois word "kanata," which means village. Cartier modified this to "Canada" to refer to the entire area governed by their chief.

Settlement

Joao Alvarez Fagundes, a Portuguese navigator, sometime between 1520 and 1525, attempted a settlement at Ingonish on Cape Breton Island, Nova Scotia. It failed within a year to a year and a half. A French knight, the Sieur de Roberval, in 1541 also tried to found a colony, but this attempt was abandoned ten years later, and without the diamonds or gold the knight had hoped to find. Another French nobleman, Pierre du Gua, Sieur de Monts, would have better success. Accompanied by the skilled mapmaker Samuel de Champlain, in 1604 he sailed up Passamaquoddy Bay and established a settlement on Saint Croix Island in the Saint Croix River, which forms part of the boundary between New Brunswick and Maine. The colonists survived only one winter on the island, but the effort did not die. They were able to relocate to a more favorable site across the Bay of Fundy at Port Royal, in what is now Nova Scotia, near the present town of Annapolis Royal.

Actually, the question might be raised as to whether the Saint Croix colony was a pioneer Canadian community or in reality an American one. During the War of 1812 the island was considered neutral territory where the adversaries could meet to discuss matters. Eventually a full-fledged boundary dispute broke out, and both the United States and Britain's New Brunswick colony claimed Saint Croix Island. In 1842 the United States successfully annexed it. The importance of Saint Croix to Canadian history was finally officially recognized in 1982 when the governments of the United States, Canada, and New Brunswick entered into an agreement to recognize it as the "Saint Croix Island International Historic Site." Parks Canada and the United States National Park Service each maintain small interpretive sites on their respective shores of the Saint Croix River.

Later efforts by other Frenchmen would also be successful, but not without undergoing difficulty. Samuel de Champlain established Place Royal (Quebec City) in 1608, although most of the original settlers died within a year. Montreal was settled in 1642, with the help of the Jesuits, who had been active in what was known as New France since 1625.

Although the French settlements in Quebec may have been the most prominent, the British and French both undertook similar efforts elsewhere. Temporary French fish camps existed on the Ferryland coast of Newfoundland as early as 1504. A 1585 British attempt to settle on the site of St. John's failed, but in 1610 John Guy of Bristol established a chartered colony at Cupids on Conception Bay. In 1627 George Calvert, Lord Baltimore, would be successful in founding his Avalon colony at Ferryland, south of St. John's. Today visitors can "return" to that pioneer effort by viewing the archeological excavations and the excellent, interpretive exhibits in the modern visitors center.

As we have noted, the first French settlers arrived at St. Croix Island in 1604, spent one winter there, and then relocated to Nova Scotia. Known as the Acadians, they resided in an area hotly contested by both Britain and France, and one that changed hands numerous times. Desiring only to be left in peace they would be here until expelled by the British in 1755, along with expulsion from Prince Edward Island in 1758. Some would flee into the interior, escaping into the more remote areas of Nova Scotia and also into New Brunswick and Quebec, but most were forced to leave the entire Maritime area and were deported to New England, England, France, and elsewhere. Their plight was made famous in Henry Wadsworth Longfellow's poem *Evangeline*. Eventually many made their way to Louisiana, which at the time was French territory. Their descendents are the present day Cajuns.

At least indirectly, France established more formal control over Canada in 1627. Advisor to the Bourbon monarchy, the powerful Cardinal Richelieu granted New France to a group known as the Company of 100 Associates. Within a few years the French began the lucrative fur trade in earnest. Ironically a lack of interest on the part of the Bourbons led to two Frenchmen and their associates approaching the British to charter the Hudson's Bay Company. The charter granted in 1670 created the oldest continuously incorporated company in the world. The company would dominate the fur trade and essentially be the government in most of what is now Western Canada for two centuries. From 1783 until 1821 it did have a serious rival in the North West Company, but in the later year the two concerns merged. In 1870 the Hudson's Bay Company would cede the huge expense of land it controlled in Western and Northern Canada, an area known as Rupert's Land, to the government of Canada. It would continue in the fur trade for some years, and today operates sophisticated, modern department stores in Canada's largest cities.

British Rule

Outside Newfoundland, there were some attempts by the British to colonize in the Maritimes, especially Nova Scotia. The first in that province was an unsuccessful 1629 effort to settle at Port Royal, site of an earlier French fort. France and Britain would continue to struggle over possession of the area for more than a century. In 1749 the British founded Halifax, and it was clear they were here to stay. The old fortress of the Citadel in the heart of the modern city serves witness to that. The Treaty of Paris in 1763, ending the Seven Years War, went on to give London uncontested control over all of Canada.

Although British sovereignty was clear, outside the towns of what had been New France and an outpost such as Halifax, there were few European settlers anywhere in Canada. The American Revolution would change that. Few citizens of the United States seem to realize that this country's battle to be free of King George III was hardly a unanimous one. Estimates claim that fully 40 percent of the residents in the original Thirteen Colonies could be labeled Loyalists to the British Crown. Some undoubtedly stayed, probably because they felt they had no real alternative. Others saw Canada as a place of refuge. It is not surprising that Canadian political culture has traditionally stressed elements such as peace and order. The country was partially founded on such principles. Loyalists poured over the border into New Brunswick, Nova Scotia, and Ontario during and after the Revolution and in certain cases up to fifteen years before. This was not an easy journey for many, and some failed to survive the first winter in their chosen northern home.

The Revolution did not always remain behind. For a time American rebels seized part of Montreal, and tried unsuccessfully to take the walled city of Quebec. Revolutionaries in Maine launched a raid into Nova Scotia, which also had among its residents sympathizers to the cause as well as Loyalists. During the War of 1812 the now independent Americans attacked and burned Fort York (Toronto) and expected to ultimately occupy all of Canada. British retaliation led to the burning of the White House and an unsuccessful effort to capture Baltimore's Fort McHenry. Perhaps in the first conflict the Americans had hoped for support from the mostly French populace. It never came. Britain had wisely enacted the Quebec Act in 1774, which guaranteed to their French subjects protection for their language and religion. They in turn stayed very loyal to their new rulers.

By 1791 enough European settlers had come into the region that Britain enacted the Constitutional Act of Upper (Ontario) and Lower (Quebec) Canada. In effect this created two separate colonies each with its own legislature, while the Maritimes and Newfoundland would have their own governments. For the first time the term "Canada" was used in an official way. It may be helpful to note that Ontario was designated as Upper Canada, although it lies west and south of Quebec, because it lies further inland on the St. Lawrence River, which flows south to north. In effect Ontario is "up river." By 1837 there was enough unhappiness with the governmental situation that rebellions broke out in both colonies, especially Quebec. This led to an investigation by Lord Durham, which was rather negative toward Quebec but which also called for combining the two colonies into one with two separate provinces. The 1840 Act of Union accomplished this. Like it or not, Ontario and Quebec have lived together ever since.

Seven years later, under Lord Elgin's governorship, Britain granted responsible government to Canada. This meant Canadians were now largely in control of their own governmental affairs, and if not actual independence it was a step on the way. New Brunswick and Nova Scotia gained a similar status not long after this.

Canadian Confederation

Although the dispute between Britain and the United States over the boundary of the Oregon Territory had finally been settled in 1846 during the administration of President James Polk, old concerns of a possible American invasion were rekindled by the Civil War. British purchases of Confederate cotton and sales of ships and ammunition to the South helped to create animosity, as did a Confederate raid launched from Quebec on St. Albans, Vermont. After the war the American government tolerated raids into Canada by radical Irishmen known as Fenians who hoped to capture the colony and use it as a base in the struggle for Irish independence. These attacks would continue as late as 1871. Some American officials also talked openly of seizing Canada as part of their country's "manifest destiny." With the purchase of Alaska from Russia in 1867 the Oregon question surfaced again with renewed American interest in British Columbia.

Already by 1864 invasion fears, along with the hope of promoting more trade, led to meetings in Charlottetown, Prince Edward Island, at Province House. It was here that the concept of a united Canada was born. Delegates came from Ontario, Quebec, New Brunswick, Nova Scotia, Prince Edward Island, and Newfoundland. They would come to be known appropriately as the Fathers of Confederation.

Because of complications over land titles and other factors, Prince Edward Island would delay joining Canada until 1871, while Newfoundland, seeing little advantage to confederation and feeling quite safe from an American attack, would stay outside the union until 1949. The remaining four delegations agreed to meet a month later in Quebec. There the final details of the agreement begun at Charlottetown were reached. While Canadian leadership may have been sold on the idea of union, it was hardly a popular idea with the population at large, which often felt little would be gained and local control would be lost. New Brunswick was the only colony to hold a referendum on the matter, and a majority voted against it. Even before its birth Canada was actually a land where regional interests and loyalties were very strong.

Despite such setbacks the agreement moved forward toward reality. A railroad connecting the Maritimes to Quebec was promised as one way of making the agreement more palatable to the opposition. On March 29, 1867, Queen Victoria signed the British North America Act, which had been passed by Parliament. This was to be Canada's constitution until 1982, and in modified form still is a part of it. At noon on July 1, 1867, the Act became law. The three colonies of Canada (Ontario and Quebec), Nova Scotia, and New Brunswick were now officially the Dominion of Canada. Supposedly Queen Victoria chose Ottawa as the capital for the new dominion and selected it because it would be less subject to

American influence than the other practical choices. In reality, the city, like most large Canadian cities, is only a modest distance away from the border.

Expansion

By 1858 both Vancouver Island and British Columbia had colonial administrations. Ten years later they were merged into one. Meanwhile the Red River Colony on the prairies of Manitoba had attracted enough settlers that in 1869 Manitoba was admitted to the Confederation. Logically British Columbia received an invitation to join. She accepted and was admitted in 1870, but her price was the commitment to build a transcontinental railroad.

That railroad was the fabled Canadian Pacific. The route through the mountains was challenging. Track was not actually laid until 1880, and the last spike driven until November 7, 1885. Early surveyors had favored a more northern route through the Yellowhead Pass west of Jasper, Alberta. A more southern one through Kicking Horse Pass and Eagle Pass was finally selected, at least in part because it would help reinforce Canadian control over southern British Columbia in case the Americans ever decided to reopen the Oregon question. It was Major A. B. "Hells Bells" Rogers who found the pass which bears his name in the Selkirk Mountains that made the line possible. With lots of sweat and inspiration the railroad was completed, and British Columbia was linked to the rest of Canada. So successful was the Canadian Pacific that more railroads were started. During World War I several of these came under government ownership and were merged into the Canadian National Railways.

The government-run Canadian National operated with the private Canadian Pacific, both helping to bind the nation together, until 1995 when the Canadian National was also privatized. This Canadian tolerance for peaceful coexistence between the public and private sectors has not been limited to the rails. Government controlled CBC Radio and Television has had to compete with private stations for its audience. At times provincial governments have operated economic enterprises, usually either to minimize foreign influence or to keep a financially troubled one in business.

The tragic, unsuccessful Indian and Metis uprising led by Louis Riel in 1884-1885 was a setback for the Canadian prairies and indeed for the entire country. Still, it was not an end to Westward expansion. With the completion of the Canadian Pacific and the following of other rail lines, European immigrants now had much easier access to the Canadian interior. Railroads and steamship lines eager for business, and assisted by governments looking for hardworking settlers, advertised cheap, or in some cases free, land to those who were willing to risk everything and start a new life in a new continent. Probably the period between 1903 and 1914 was the peak of this prairie immigration. In 1905 both Alberta and Saskatchewan traded territorial for full provincial status. By that time Asian immigrants had already arrived in British Columbia, many having come to build the railroads.

Even Canada's usually sparsely populated North began to attract attention. Fortune seekers, mostly Americans outfitted in Seattle, poured into the Yukon when the Klondike Gold Rush broke out in 1896. As a result the Yukon Territory was organized in 1898 and remains one of the three territories lying to the north of the provinces. In creating the Yukon Territory out of a western portion of the Northwest Territories, Canada hoped to keep it out of the hands of the Americans, across the border in Alaska. The actual boundary between the Yukon and Alaska was in dispute until 1903, when it was finally settled on terms largely favorable to Alaska.

Modern Canada is Born

In some ways Canada came of age in World War I. Canadian casualties in both World Wars, and the size of her partially conscripted armies were high, considering the population of the country. Her early entry into World War I even brought some Americans north of the border to volunteer, since America would not enter the war until three years later.

The sacrifices were not without controversy. Quebec was unhappy with conscription, since its citizens felt that Canadian foreign and defense policy was too closely tied to that of London, nor did they want their sons to die for the mere cause of defending British colonial interests. In spite of such questions and concerns, Canada's contribution was significant. The Allies recognized this, and Canada earned herself a place at the peace conferences ending both conflicts. She would be a founding member of the League of Nations and the United Nations, although isolationist sentiments similar to those in the United States made her somewhat dubious of the League.

In nearly all ways, while the British monarch was symbolically head of Canada as well, she was a fully sovereign, independent nation. Still, there were some remaining legal ties to Britain. A dispute between Quebec and Newfoundland (which remained a separate colony) over ownership of Labrador was settled in favor of Newfoundland in a 1927 decision by the British Privy Council, which had the responsibility of ruling on disputes between British territories. In 1931 Parliament passed the Statute of Westminster, thus recognizing the full independence of all British dominions, such as Canada, including defense and foreign affairs. However, the power to amend the British North America Act continued to rest with Parliament, and in matters affecting the relationship between the federal government and the provinces would do so until 1982. Ironically Quebec was not totally unhappy with that arrangement since it provided protection from unpopular decisions by English-speaking Canada.

The Great Depression brought economic devastation to Canada, just as it did to other developed countries. Canada's West probably developed the country's two most radical efforts for trying to combat it. From Alberta William "Bible Bill" Aberhart, a popular radio preacher, launched the populist Social Credit movement. On the one hand, he denounced banks. On the other, he advocated that the government give each resident a monthly dividend of twenty-five dollars. Social Credit never was able to institute its dividend plan or reform banks according to its policies, but it was able to establish provincial governments in Alberta and British Columbia and did enact some reforms such as crop insurance. A branch of the party even managed to emerge in Quebec, where it was more concerned with Quebec nationalism than the original goals of the movement. Although technically still in existence, by the end of the 1980s the Social Credit party was for all practical purposes gone. Replacing it was the Reform party, under Preston Manning, who had in the past had been a member of Social Credit and also done some radio preaching. Manning's father, Ernest, had been a former Social Credit leader and premier of Alberta. Eventually the Reform party and the mostly Eastern Progressive Conservatives would merge into a new Conservative party.

Another clergyman, Baptist Tommy Douglas, had considerable success. During the Depression years the Cooperative Commonwealth Federation was born, and later became the New Democratic party. As we have noted, Douglas and the CCF won control of the Saskatchewan provincial government in 1944, and he would continue to serve as Premier until 1961. Having introduced free hospital care during their first term, Douglas and the New Democrats after a 1960 election victory went to work to establish a full government-sponsored health service that eventually became a model for the entire country. In 1962, under Premier Woodrow Lloyd, this medicare plan became a reality in Saskatchewan, and in 1966 was implemented throughout the entire country. In a recent survey Canadians called the now national health service the country's greatest accomplishment of the past century. The liberal-leaning New Democrats are truly a national party, even if not strong enough to form a government. They have governed in Saskatchewan and elsewhere in the West, as well as in Ontario. Today they also have some strength in Atlantic Canada, and in every national election they do manage to elect candidates to Parliament in Ottawa.

Canada, as she had done in World War I, played a significant role in World War II. Again she would participate at the peace table. A founding member of the United Nations, as the Cold War emerged she had a similar spot in the North Atlantic Treaty Organization (NATO). Despite urgings by the American government, she did resist moves to become a nuclear military power.

In 1957 two decades of Liberal party rule came to an end when Progressive Conservative John Diefenbaker was victorious and replaced

Louis St. Laurent as prime minister. Although born in Ontario, Diefenbaker grew up in Saskatchewan and in many ways really was a product of the Canadian West. His slogan for the country was "One Canada." That was popular in the Western provinces, which saw it as applying not only to equality of people throughout the country but also to equality of regions as well. His "Vision of the North," which promoted Northern economic development was also well received by many Canadians. Unfortunately Quebec saw the slightly less than six years of Diefenbaker government as a threat to the traditional view of the "Two Solitudes," or the two founding nations. Had Diefenbaker been prime minister at an earlier time, perhaps this would not have mattered. However, the times were changing, and Quebec was restless.

The 1960s saw the Quiet Revolution radically transform the francophone province. Ignoring the traditional approach of the Roman Catholic Church of retreating to the farm and an inward-looking rural way of life, young, francophone Quebecers began to gain control of the province's commercial life and to play a more active role in its political one. They were peaceful but determined. Others were not quite so peaceful. The *Front de liberation du Quebec* (FLQ) dynamited mailboxes, and in 1970 kidnapped two persons, killing one of them. While less dramatic, potentially far more threatening to Ottawa than the FLQ, was the founding in 1967 of the Parti Quebecois by Rene Levesque and other sovereignists. Parti Quebecois was not the first separatist party in Quebec's history, but it would rather rapidly turn out to be the most popular. Quebec nationalism was obviously here to stay. Even those committed to federalism and remaining in Canada felt that major changes needed to be made in the relationship.

Some of these changes first appeared in the 1960s. Liberal party leader Lester Pearson became prime minister in 1963 and moved to replace the traditional Canadian flag, which consisted of the British Red Ensign, with the Union Jack, along with the Canadian coat of arms (the Union Jack is still found in several of the provincial flags). After much discussion and disagreement, in 1965 the now well-known Maple Leaf flag replaced the older standard. It features a red maple leaf against a white background along with a vertical red stripe on each end. Red and white have been

Canada's national colors since 1921. The maple leaf has long been a traditional Canadian symbol, while the two stripes symbolize the Atlantic and Pacific Oceans and convey the concept that Canada stretches from one sea to the other. If controversial at first, the Maple Leaf has become so widely accepted by Canadians that there was much unhappiness when it was accidentally flown upside down at the Atlanta Summer Olympics. Clearly, symbols can be important.

If a new flag was one step toward creating a Canada that could more successfully unite its diverse peoples, dynamic Liberal party Prime Minister Pierre Trudeau took another. His government in 1969 passed the Official Language Act. This law made Canada formally bilingual at the national, but not the provincial level. The act has not been without its critics. One British Columbia businessman was quoted as being tired of reading French on his cereal boxes. It has also had its benefits and supporters. Many of Canada's younger people in particular have or are achieving bilingualism in both English and French. Even sovereignists usually recognize the importance of knowing English for business purposes and encourage it as a second language in the schools of Quebec. Bilingualism could have economic benefits for Canada in the future, although it does add to the expense of government and education.

Outside the schools, things sometimes seemed to be going in a different direction at the provincial level. In 1976 for the first time the Parti Quebecois came into power, and Rene Levesque, as head of the party, was now the provincial premier. In a move that it felt essential to preserve Quebec's culture, The Levesque government wasted no time in enacting into law the Charter of the French Language in 1977. This and related legislation would give French a legally recognized status in the province, requiring its use in business and increasing its importance in the schools. A series of controversial statutes finally resulted in a language law that permits public signs in languages other than English but only if the same sign includes the French text in larger letters.

By 1980 the Parti Quebecois felt strong enough to hold a referendum on separation from Canada. Actually it advocated what Levesque referred to as sovereignty-association, which would have separated Quebec politically from Canada but left it linked economically. The referendum failed, with 60 percent voting no, and possibly many Canadians thought the question was settled for some time. Such was not the case.

Pierre Trudeau had served as prime minister from 1968 to 1978. In 1980 he and the Liberal party were again voted into power, and Trudeau would continue as prime minister in 1984. On the whole he was a popular leader, although not without his adversaries, including sovereignists from his native Quebec and a rather paranoid FBI, which considered him some sort of Marxist sympathizer and potential leftist threat. A champion of the right of Canadian nationalities to use their own language and preserve their culture, he was just as staunch a federalist. In a bold effort to help create a Canada where all nationalities would be equal but protected, Trudeau took the cause of patriation of the Constitution to the provinces. Patriation would mean the British Parliament in London would give up its right to approve amendments to the Canadian Constitution, thus severing the last formal legal link between the two countries, although the British monarch would still remain monarch of Canada, as long as Canada desired.

It might seem that such a move by a prime minister from Quebec would be overwhelmingly welcomed in his native province. French and English Canadians would appear to be placed on a more equal footing, since the existing constitution, the British North America Act, 1867 (also referred to as the Constitution Act, 1867) was in reality an act or law passed by the British Parliament. While Quebec would certainly welcome ending technical control of the Constitution by London, it could do so only if the customary protection against arbitrary action by the English-speaking majority, London's necessary approval provided, could be maintained. There was also a traditional understanding that significant changes would not be requested without the consent of both founding nations. The proposed document, while requiring the unanimous approval of all provinces for certain future changes, permitted other changes with less than unanimous agreement. Quebec objected. When the government decided to go ahead with patriation regardless of Quebec's protests, Quebecers felt they were victims of the "Night of Long Knives." Despite the objections, the British Parliament enacted the text submitted to it, thus giving up forever the right to control Canadian affairs, a right which by this time had long fallen into disuse. The Constitution Act, 1982, went into effect on April 17.

Although it has employed one provision of the Constitution to frustrate the federal Supreme Court, Quebec has never formally ratified the document. Conservative party Prime Minister Brian Mulroney, also from Quebec, made two valiant but unsuccessful attempts to end the Constitutional crisis. The first, the 1987 Meech Lake Accord, would have recognized Quebec as a "distinct society." Although passed by the Quebec Legislature, it required the approval of all ten provinces, and was rejected in Manitoba and Newfoundland (which reversed an earlier favorable vote). The second, the 1992 Charlottetown Accord, which sought to address Western grievances as well as those of Quebec, was put to a national referendum. It was defeated in most provinces including Quebec. The Constitutional crisis continues to the present day.

By 1995 Parti Quebecois, firmly in control of the provincial government, felt the time was ripe for a second referendum. The skillful and popular leader Lucien Bouchard took over during the campaign as party head and provincial premier. He almost succeeded. Quebec voters rejected separation by about 1 percent of the votes cast. The question they were asked to approve or refuse was so vaguely worded that some undoubtedly believed they were simply endorsing negotiations with the federal government on Quebec's grievances. Still, the results were rather clear. In business-oriented Montreal, and the Ottawa valley, with its high-tech industry and close proximity to the federal capital, there was considerable opposition. Elsewhere in most cases a majority of francophones voted yes. The votes of the English-speaking minority, native peoples, and immigrants were overwhelmingly opposed, and that is all that prevented victory for the sovereignists. Some Canadians now saw the breakup of the country as only a matter of time.

It is unfortunate that the Quebec crisis so dominated Canadian politics in the last two decades of the twentieth century that nearly everything else seems to have been forgotten. Much was accomplished, including even some possible progress on the Constitutional question. After the referendum, at the urging of New Brunswick Premier Frank McKenna, the leaders of all Canadian provinces and territories other than Quebec met to deal with the problem. Their work ultimately led to the signing of the Calgary Agreement in Calgary, Alberta, on September 14, 1997. Although dismissed by the Parti Quebecois, the pact, which was ultimately unanimously approved by the provincial and territorial legislatures other than Quebec, may at some future date be the basis for settling the Constitutional question. It seeks to answer Quebec's concerns by recognizing "the unique character of Quebec society. At the same time it attempted to alleviate Western unhappiness by declaring that all provinces have "equality of status" and should have equal rights under the Constitution.

Even in Quebec there seemed to be a change in mood by the late 1990s. It may have been the result of exhaustion over the referendum process more than an abandonment of the dream of becoming a separate nation. However, polls repeatedly uncovered solid majorities opposing separation and even greater ones against holding a third referendum. The 2001 election for the federal Parliament saw the Liberal party make substantial gains against the separatist Bloc Quebecois, who represent the sovereignists in Ottawa much the same way as the Parti Quebecois does at the provincial level. In June 2004 the Bloc retook many of those seats at the expense of former Prime Minister Paul Martin's Liberal government, and it continued to do well in the 2006 federal election. This seemed to be more the result of unhappiness with the Liberal party rather than a dramatic resurgence of separatist longings.

If the possibilities for holding the country together seemed to grow brighter, so did its economic situation. Conservative party provincial party premiers such as Ralph Klein in Alberta and Mike Harris in Ontario took major steps to cut spending and balance budgets. Other provinces also moved in the same direction. There were cries of alarm that the cuts were too deep and too fast, with damage done to both health care and education. Undoubtedly there was some, but on the whole the country appeared stronger and more prosperous as it put its economic house in order. The governing Liberal party under Prime Minister Jean Chretien made similar and successful, if somewhat less drastic, efforts to reduce federal spending. Paul Martin, as prime minister, pledged to work for the end of trade disputes with the United States, and Stephen Harper's government brought about a settlement of the dispute over importation of Canadian softwood lumber. Indeed Canadian prosperity and the country's social welfare safety net at one time earned it the designation by a United Nations organization as the world's best country in which to live. Perhaps that is why it has become so attractive to immigrants from every continent. Canadians will admit to paying higher taxes than in the United States, but many would also claim they get good value for their dollars with more services, including government-funded health care.

On the international scene Canada was also playing a prominent role. Its military took part in Desert Storm in the Middle East and also participated in a number of peacekeeping operations. Diplomatically Ottawa made headlines as it led a successful effort that resulted in the 1997 signing of a treaty in Oslo, Norway, by over one hundred nations to ban the use of land mines. Enough signatories have since formally ratified the treaty for it to go into effect. Every year mines kill and maim thousands of people, most civilians, while increasingly from a military standpoint their usage is questionable. Lady Diana Spencer worked tirelessly for an end to their use until her death. The treaty while still unsigned by Russia, China, and the United States is, nevertheless, a major step in that direction.

In 1988 Canada signed the Free Trade Agreement with the United States, which in 1993 was expanded to include Mexico and become the North American Free Trade Agreement. The Canadian economy was large enough to also earn the country membership in the influential G-8 group of nations. Their meetings to a certain extent have the power to impact the economy of the entire planet.

As the new millennium became a reality, Canada was one of the countries clearly in a position to play a constructive role in the future of the world's political and economic relations. If its multi nationalism was a challenge, it also gave the country a rich storehouse of diversity that could serve it well no matter with whom or where it may be dealing. Such countries, if they have the vision and courage, may claim the future as their own.

CANADIAN GOVERNMENT IN A NUTSHELL

Our Grand Tour and journey back in time should help us better understand how Canadians govern themselves. Some things may look familiar, as Canadians have borrowed ideas from both the United States and Britain, but other factors are truly Canadian. They may not work in either Britain or America, but they do work here, because Canada has a blend of geography, history, and culture which is uniquely its own.

The Constitution

If you go to a library and ask a librarian to help you find a copy of the British Constitution, after a few hours a frustrated staff will probably tell you to leave and never return. The reason is simple. Britain has no single written document known as the constitution. Yet the opening statement in the original Canadian Constitution, the British North America Act, 1867, says it is the desire of Canada to have a constitution similar to that of the United Kingdom. In reality the British Constitution does exist, and in certain ways that of Canada does resemble it. The great British Parliamentarian Edmund Burke declared that his nation's constitution "existed time out of mind." That is it evolved over the centuries. Some parts of it, such as the Magna Carta, the Petition of Right, and the Act of Union do exist in written form. Others rest simply on custom and tradition. Burke knew that the real strength of a constitution was not whether it was written or not but whether it was believed. Few citizens in the former Soviet Union took that country's constitutional bill of rights very seriously, although it was written down for anyone to read.

Some aspects of Canadian constitutional government, like the British, rest on tradition or conventions. In both countries it is simply understood that if the prime minister and his or her political party lose a vote (a vote of confidence) on a government-sponsored bill in the House of Commons, the prime minister and all other government ministers will resign. An election will follow shortly. While no-confidence votes are rare in either country, just the possibility of one is a check on the abuse of governmental power. Actually the entire idea of a prime minister and cabinet ministers responsible to a larger parliamentary body really evolved out of the English governmental experience. No one sat down and decided that this was the way things should be done. Both Canada and Britain have found that for them this system works quite well. Although Canada thus shares certain common governmental roots with Britain, unlike that country it does indeed have a written constitution.

Today the formal constitution of Canada is the Canada Act, 1982, which in a technical sense was an act of the British Parliament, and one in which it permanently gave up its right to pass future legislation of any kind for its one-time dominion. The Canada Act actually contains two constitutional documents and their amendments, the British North America Act, 1867 (also known as the Constitution Act, 1867) and the Constitution Act, 1982. Canada's first constitution, the British North America Act, was not abolished with the passage of the second. Instead, the second one adds to it and in places modifies and clarifies it. The basic fundamentals of the Canadian constitutional system are found in both documents and in the governmental conventions inherited from Britain and evolving throughout the country's history.

Undoubtedly in creating the new nation the Fathers of Confederation were influenced by their powerful neighbor to the south. Like the United States, Canada is one of the few genuinely federal nations in the world, with a constitutional separation of power between the central government and the member provinces. A federal arrangement works well in large countries like the United States, Canada, and Australia with a variety of geography and regional cultures. Because of their fear of the American Civil War the Fathers of Confederation reserved unspecified powers to the federal government, just the opposite of the system in the United States. While now fallen into disuse, the federal government even had the power to disallow or delay provincial legislation it did not like. Despite these Constitutional provisions, regional loyalties and interests are far stronger in Canada than in the United States, where they have gradually diminished in the years following the Civil War. Like American states, Canadian provinces are permitted their own constitutions.

In the Canadian system certain powers do rest with the federal government that are at least partially under the states here. Recent years may have seen some dilution of federal authority in such areas, but for the most part criminal law, banking, and interest rates are within the federal jurisdiction. Education and health care are provincial responsibilities, but the provincial government health services could not survive without federal financial assistance. Both Ottawa and the provinces have power in such areas as agriculture and immigration, while the taxing authority of the federal government is greater than that at the provincial level.

Although federalism has usually served Canada and the United States well, the history of both countries does furnish examples of the almost inevitable tension that occasionally arises in such governmental systems. In 1970 federal Prime Minister Trudeau was insistent that a new airport be constructed just east of Toronto to handle traffic from Europe, and much land was expropriated for that purpose. P.O.P, People or Planes, organized to protest this project. Ontario Premier Bill Davis put a permanent halt to it when he informed the federal government that while it had the Constitutional right to construct the airport, the Province of Ontario would build no roads to service it.

The Crown

The Constitution establishes the British Crown as also the Crown in Canada and head of government. The Crown rests in the reigning British monarch. Canadians could of course abolish the symbol of monarchy anytime they wish, but many prefer to keep it or are at least indifferent about it. The monarch's portrait has traditionally appeared on the currency of the nation as a result. Since usually the monarch is not resident in Canada, she, or he, is officially represented by a person known as the Governor General. There is also a royal representative in each of the provinces who is known as the Lieutenant Governor. Britain selected the Governor General until 1936. Since 1952 the Governor General has always been a Canadian citizen.

Technically the signature of either the monarch or the Governor General is necessary before a bill becomes law. In reality approval of legislation passed by Parliament is never withheld. The monarch is a symbol and ceremonial leader who does not formulate government policy. Any political addresses given by the Governor General would in reality be presentations of the current government's positions and policies. Real political power does not lie in the institution of the Crown but elsewhere. The Crown's power is to serve as a symbol of the nation and of an important aspect of its heritage.

Today, especially among Canada's younger citizens, interest in the monarch appears to be in considerable decline. Surveys indicate that only about 50 percent of the total population still supports the concept of monarchy for the country, although in provinces such as British Columbia and Ontario the figure is approximately 60 percent. As might be expected, Quebec is considerably lower, with less than 30 percent desiring to retain the institution. Canadians did widely and enthusiastically commemorate Queen Elizabeth II's Golden Jubilee in 2002 and her visit to their country. They also minted a complete set of the nation's coins to commemorate the event. However, for some the celebration of Elizabeth's reign may have been as much because they admire her personally than because she is their queen. Interestingly enough, also in 2002 the government issued a new ten-dollar banknote without the customary portrait of the reigning monarch. This change was met with indifference on the part of the population. Increasingly Canadians, regardless of their ancestry, are probably more interested in creating and identifying with symbols that come out of their own experience and culture rather than someone else's history. The symbol of the monarch may not totally disappear, but it seems destined to gradually fade into the background.

Parliament

Canada is a nation with a parliamentary form of government. In certain ways the Canadian Parliament does resemble the United States Congress, but in other ways it is quite different. Often it appears similar to the British Parliament, but at times it is strictly Canadian. All three assemblies are the supreme law-making bodies in their respective countries. They also are bicameral, or have two houses. However, unlike the powerful United States Senate, the British House of Lords and the Canadian Senate are politically rather weak bodies. Neither Britain nor Canada shares the American love affair with separation of powers or checks and balances, although Canada, through its Supreme Court and its Constitutional Charter of Rights and Freedoms, more closely resembles the United States in this aspect than does the government in London. All of this will become clearer as we take a brief look at the major Canadian governmental institutions.

The Senate

The upper chamber of the Canadian Parliament is known as the Senate. In one way it is modeled on the British House of Lords, as it is not an elected body. Unlike Lords, no one with a seat in the Senate holds a title of nobility. (In 2001 the British government enacted legislation modernizing the House of Lords and drastically reducing the number of members who sit there by virtue of a hereditary title of nobility. All those with life peerages are still entitled to their seats.) On several occasions Canadian governmental officials and other leading national figures have declared such designations are not in keeping with Canadian tradition or culture. Senators must live in the province that they represent, and are selected by the prime minister, not the provincial government, a system that Western Canada in particular feels is obsolete. Originally they served for life or until they resigned. Now they must retire at seventy-five.

The American Senate provides equal representation to each state. Canada's Senate was intended to do that for the major regions of the country. Unfortunately, as the nation has changed and population growth has increased dramatically in the West, major inequality has been the actual result. Ontario and Quebec each receive twenty-four Senators. The Maritimes have twenty-four, while the Western provinces of Alberta, British Columbia, Saskatchewan, and Manitoba must share twenty-four. When Newfoundland joined the Confederation in 1949 she was given six, while each of the three territories has one, making a total of 105. This situation results in two small provinces, New Brunswick and Nova Scotia, having ten Senators each, while rapidly growing and economically powerful Alberta and British Columbia each have only six, just two more than Prince Edward Island, the smallest province. If you add Newfoundland's six to the Maritimes twenty-four, Atlantic Canada becomes even more over represented with a total of thirty seats.

Calls for Senate reform are strong in the West. The Charlottetown Accord, which failed to gain approval in a national referendum, would have brought in the so-called Triple-E Senate. More similar to its American counterpart, this Senate would have had an equal number of Senators from each province, been popularly elected, and had effective control over passage of legislation with the lower house, the House of Commons. If the electorate had been voting on Senate reform alone, quite possibly it would have passed.

Technically the Senate is equal to the House of Commons. Its approval is needed for the passage of all legislation. In reality, since it is not an elected body it is expected to give way to the House of Commons if the two chambers cannot agree. That is normally the case in such instances. If a possible deadlock does develop the prime minister has the power to select an additional four or eight Senators, with an equal number coming from each region.

Some Senators have been accused of not taking their job very seriously. Clearly the body does not effectively represent regional interests today. Unlike the House of Commons, it cannot force a government out with a vote of no confidence. The vast majority of Senators have come only from the Liberal and Conservative parties, since every Canadian prime minister has been from one or the other of those two parties. Almost everyone agrees reform is needed, including the present Conservative government, which has proposed giving the electorate some choice in Senate selection. That is easier said than done. Every proposed reform means the loss of power by someone. Few are eager to walk away from it voluntarily. Because of these factors, the Senate normally plays only a minor role in the nation's daily political life.

The House of Commons and the Prime Minister

As in Great Britain, in Canada you find actual Parliamentary power in the House of Commons. It is similar to the United States House of Representatives in that candidates run from single-member districts, which in Canada are known as ridings, and can be elected by a simple plurality of the votes cast. Unlike the House of Representatives, the number of seats is not permanently fixed but is adjusted every twenty years after a national census has been taken. There are 308 Members of Parliament in the House, which means on average each MP represents approximately 86,000 Canadians. Candidates do not have to be residents of the ridings they wish to represent, although many are. Ontario, with the largest population, has the most seats. Quebec follows with seventy-five. The Constitution guarantees no province will have fewer than it had in 1976 or fewer than the number of Senators it possesses. This entitles Prince Edward Island to four seats. Each of the three territories receives one. As a result of the 2001 census, Ontario gained three seats, going from 103 to 106, and Alberta and British Columbia an additional two each. This brought the new total from 301 to the present 308. An election for the House must be held at least every five years, but as we shall see, one normally occurs about every four.

There is a Speaker of the House, who unlike his American counterpart, is expected to serve as a politically neutral parliamentarian. Actual political leadership is the responsibility of the prime minister. Since there is no separation of powers, the prime minister must be a Member of Parliament. He or she (Kim Campbell was Canada's first woman prime minister in 1993) is always from the House of Commons. While the President of the United States is elected by the entire electorate which votes for a college of electors, the only Canadians who actually cast ballots for the prime minister are those voting in the riding in which the prime minister is running for Parliament. The leader of the party who wins the most seats becomes the prime minister. The party with the second highest number of seats is officially recognized as the opposition.

The prime minister's party will form the government. If this party does not have a majority of the seats in the House, it could form a coalition government with another party, but such arrangements, although not unknown, are rare in Canada. Minority governments that do not have an absolute majority of the seats occur more frequently and are not necessarily unstable. After the June 2004 election Prime Minister Paul Martin and the Liberals successfully formed such a government. The Conservative government elected in 2006 and under the leadership of Stephen Harper is similar. The prime minister selects members of the government party to serve as heads of the various departments of the government. At least one will come from the Senate. These persons are known as ministers, and the more important ones will serve in the prime minister's cabinet. The prime minister determines which government ministries are important enough to warrant cabinet status. Some such as Finance, National Defence, and External Affairs and International Trade are so important they will always be included regardless of who is currently prime minister. Unlike the American Cabinet, which rarely meets collectively, the Canadian Prime Minister and Cabinet have regularly scheduled meetings to discuss and formulate policy.

Although individual Members of Parliament, including those of the government party, and opposition parties may introduce legislation, almost all important legislation is introduced by the government ministers and originates in the various ministries. The House has committees, which may review and revise legislation, but they are not nearly as powerful as in the United States Congress.

Final votes on government-sponsored bills are strictly along party lines. This means that if a party has a true majority government, while its legislation might be amended or even withdrawn if strong opposition is sensed, should the prime minister and government insist on a final vote, the legislation will pass. On the rare occasions when this would not happen it would mean a vote of no confidence. The prime minister and all other ministers would immediately offer their resignations to the Governor General, and an election would shortly follow. Prime ministers may ask for the dissolving of Parliament at any time and thus force an election. Normally they have done this approximately every four years rather than wait until forced to do so after the passage of five. Occasionally one may be called sooner if the prime minister thinks this is in the government party's best interest.

Parliamentary systems offer certain advantages. They can be very efficient and provide the government the opportunity to do what it said it wanted to do. Ultimately the government must run on its record, and the electorate knows it always has the opposition party, or "shadow government" available as an alternative if it is unhappy. If something were to go really seriously wrong a vote of no confidence in the House could become a reality. There is no need for a long debilitating and dividing impeachment process.

Parliamentary systems also provide only the most limited checks of government power on a day-to-day basis. An appointed Senate offers little in the way of limitations, and a no vote by the Senate would at best only defeat a bill, not result in a vote of no confidence and a government resignation. Strict party voting does offer support and efficiency, but at the price of making regional representation difficult. In rare instances Canadian political parties have agreed to permit their individual members to vote either their own conscience or the view of their constituency, as was the case on both the abortion and capital punishment issues, but this is not the norm. Question period, a daily event when Parliament is in session, can force the prime minister or another government minister to publicly defend the government's policy on a particular matter. Used wisely, it is a very effective tool.

In the end every political system must decide which form of government is best whether it be a presidential system, a parliamentary one, or even an absolute monarchy, as in the case of Saudi Arabia. Undoubtedly Canada chose the parliamentary form because that is what Great Britain used. However, a fully independent Canada has chosen to retain that system of government, and the reason cannot entirely be just because it has become habitual. Parliamentary government has served it well. Canada is indeed a land of "peace, order, and good government." Most Canadians like it that way. Even Quebec's sovereignists are not urging the abolishment of the parliamentary system. If parliamentary systems have their shortcomings, so do presidential ones, where power can become fragmented and a government suffer from paralysis or regional pork-barrel interests. No system is perfect. What works best in one country may not in another.

Provincial Legislatures

In addition to the federal Parliament in Ottawa, each province and territory has its own legislative assembly headed by a premier. These bodies function at the provincial level in a fashion similar to the federal one. Quebec abolished its second chamber in 1968, and since that time all provincial and territorial legislatures have been unicameral, or one-house. British Columbia permits recall elections for the removal of unsatisfactory provincial legislators who have served at least eighteen months. Some Western residents of Canada would like to see recall adopted at the federal and provincial levels.

Several provinces are also giving serious consideration to some sort of electoral system of proportional representation that they feel would be more equitable. Under the present system candidates are elected with a simple plurality. The proportional representation proposals would distribute seats based on the percentage of votes each party achieved.

The Supreme Court and the Charter of Rights and Freedoms

Technically the Supreme Court Act, 1949, is an act of Parliament. In reality it should be considered part of Canada's Constitution, as it establishes the principles for the highest court in the land. Canada has had a Supreme Court since 1875, but until 1949 it was possible to appeal cases to the Judicial Committee of Britain's Privy Council. Today such appeals are not permitted. The Supreme Court is normally an appellate court, with cases coming before it usually having already been appealed in a lower court. Unlike its American equivalent, in rare instances the government may refer a particular question to it and request a judicial opinion. Prime Minister Jean Chretien made use of this approach to obtain a decision on what grounds the federal government would have to negotiate with Quebec in the event a future referendum received a favorable vote for sovereignty.

The Supreme Court Act calls for the prime minister to select nine judges. Again increasingly there are calls for more influence by the provinces in the selection process. By law three of the justices must be from Quebec. By convention three are from Ontario, two from the West, and one from the Atlantic Provinces.

Constitutional changes in 1982 have made Canada's highest court far more influential than before. In parliamentary systems the parliamentary body is normally considered supreme, subject to any constitutional limitations. In Britain the latest act of the country's Parliament may be considered the latest amendment to its Constitution. Canada's Constitution Act, 1982, includes an extensive Charter of Rights and Freedoms, along with an additional section on the rights of native peoples, Indians, Metis, and Inuit. It further commits the government to make monetary equalization payments to provinces that need them in order to assist them in bringing their standard of living and opportunity up to the more affluent ones. Still an additional factor is the

Constitutional right of the federal government or a province to exercise the "notwithstanding" clause, which permits it to suspend by legislative act some, but not all, of the rights, for a period up to five years. All of these modifications have created the inevitable legal questions and disputes. The result has been the need and opportunity for the Supreme Court to render judicial decisions that in effect are interpretations of the meaning of the Constitution. At this point in its history it appears to be moving closer in function to that of the American Supreme Court.

Political Parties

Most parliamentary systems tend to produce more than two parties. Canada is no exception, but from the very beginning two have dominated. Every prime minister has been either a member of the Liberal or the Conservative party, which in the early 1940s changed its name to the Progressive Conservatives. By Canadian standards both can be considered centrist parties, with of course the Liberals somewhat moderately to the left and the Conservatives to the right of the political spectrum. Both are also national parties, although historically, with certain exceptions, the Conservatives have not done well in Quebec. The Conservatives, with their traditional ties to the business community, were originally the party associated with protective tariffs to help Canada's industrial concerns. Yet, it was this party which took the lead in bringing Canada into the Free Trade Agreement with the United States. The Liberals, concerned that this treaty might open the floodgate to a major outpouring of American films, magazines, and other products that would threaten Canadian culture, at first were not enthusiastic about the Free Trade Agreement. Today both of these parties, along with most of the others, are firmly in support of it.

The New Democratic party, which emerged out of the Saskatchewan-based Cooperative Commonwealth Federation that Tommy Douglas first brought to power, has grown into a national party. Popular with some trade-union members this party can be considered the most liberal of any in the country. At one time some of its adherents advocated a kind of non-Marxist socialism, but the party has moderated past positions and certainly would not want to do anything to jeopardize the Canadian economy. At the same time it has maintained its traditional concerns for the welfare of ordinary residents of the country. While the New Democrats have been able to govern several provinces, such as Saskatchewan, British Columbia, and Ontario, they have not gathered enough support to form a national government. They have even less strength in Quebec than do the Conservatives. In federal elections most votes in that province that do not go to the separatists go to the Liberals, who often also tend to do very well in heavily-populated Ontario.

Since the twentieth century Canada has had several parties who were active in federal elections but tended to have a regional base. In the late 1980s Reform, led by Alberta's Preston Manning, became the champion of Western grievances and began to cut into support traditionally belonging to the Conservatives and Liberals. While in certain ways the most socially conservative of all of Canada's federal parties, it did well throughout the entire West because in the eyes of many in that part of the country no one else was sensitive to their interests.

In 1999, the Reform party, hoping to transform itself into a genuine national party officially dissolved itself and was resurrected into the Canadian Reform and Conservative Alliance, commonly called the Alliance for short. The hope was that the Progressive Conservatives, who had not recovered from a disastrous 1993 defeat to the Liberals, would join with it to form a new right-of -center party capable of ending Liberal rule. Originally only a few Conservatives expressed interest, while leadership disagreements in the post-Manning era continued to hurt the Alliance. Although it was still the dominant party in the West in the 2000 federal election, it won only a very small number of seats in Ontario and none at all further east. Nevertheless, efforts toward some sort of agreement continued.

October 2003 did turn out to be a dramatic time of transformation for the Alliance and for the Progressive Conservatives as well. After sometimes-difficult negotiations the two parties announced an agreement to merge into a new one. It was to be known as the united Conservative Party of Canada, have a base of support throughout the entire country, and be strong enough to give the Liberals a serious challenge. It was able to contest the June 2004 parliamentary election and came to power in the 2006 election. Canada appears to be reverting back to its traditional party system based on two national ones augmented by several others that are often more regionally based.

Bloc Quebecois is the voice of the sovereignists in Ottawa. Originally most of its Members of Parliament were disaffected Liberals who felt after the failure to resolve the Constitutional crisis separation was the only reality for Quebec's future. This is a party that ultimately hoped to successfully put itself out of business. As sovereignty for Quebec failed to materialize, the party has tended to broaden its interests and concerns and will sometimes propose policies on a variety of matters that it feels would benefit the province and perhaps the entire country. So far Bloc Quebecois has not chosen to merge itself with the Parti Quebecois, which has been powerful enough to govern Quebec at the provincial level. It has no support and seeks none outside Quebec.

In addition to Parti Quebecois, which has been a dominant force in Quebec's politics and government since the 1970s, from time to time various other parties emerge that limit their interests to a single province or territory. Among the strongest of these in recent years have been L'Action democratique du Quebec, anglophone-oriented Alliance Quebec, the Saskatchewan party, and the Yukon party. There is even the pro-independence, anti-gun registration Separation Party of Alberta, and the United Labrador Movement, which in the technical sense may not be a party but sometimes functions like one in its efforts to create a province or territory distinct from Newfoundland.

While the major federal parties do function at the provincial level, links between the federal and provincial leadership are even more tenuous than in the case of American national parties and their state equivalents, where often they are far from strong. Provincial leaders and governments pretty much establish their own policies and goals. At the city or municipal level, most candidates if not running as independents or nonpartisan, are affiliated with local parties rather than federal or provincial ones. The United States once had similar "city parties," but today the only one remaining is the Liberal party of New York.

As in both Britain and the United States, frequently new party movements will emerge in Canada at either the federal or provincial level. Some are serious attempts, while others, such as the former Rhinoceros party, are more light-hearted. Generally they tend to be about as long lasting and successful as their American equivalents.

Presidential political systems normally produce two-party politics, while parliamentary ones are often multiparty. Canada has had some elements of both. Traditionally the Liberals and Conservatives dominated. With the 1993 collapse of the Conservatives for a time the country appeared more multiparty, with the various parties each having a regional source of strength. Now we may be swinging back to a true two-party system, with additional regional and even national parties playing something of a supporting role.

Peace, Order, and Strong Government

Canadian political institutions may indeed demonstrate just how much they are *not* like us. Many folks in England might reach a similar conclusion. There are certain aspects of the Canadian political system that would leave Americans uncomfortable. Some, such as the Senate, even many Canadians think are in need of updating. Yet, there is no denying this system has served the country well. For seven years in a row Canada finished first over all other countries in the United Nations Development Program's annual human development index. In the years when it has not been at the top, it has usually been close to it, although ranking somewhat lower on certain scales within the index. While such studies can be over emphasized, this one would at least seem to indicate that the Canadian government does provide a quality of life which overall is as good as any found around the world.

No political plan is perfect. Every system occasionally needs fine tuning, but throughout their history Canadians have indeed enjoyed a high degree of "peace, order, and strong government." There is every reason to believe that the future will bring more of the same.

SO, THAT IS A CANADIAN!

Perhaps, almost without anyone realizing it, this unique mix of geography, history, and government has been blended together to create a unique people. The fact that many of them share a common language with Britain and America, and their government, like that of Britain and America, is democratically elected does not change this. They are not British. They are not American. They are truly Canadian, a people all their own. If we conclude that, then what seems to be distinctive about them, that sets them apart from other nations?

Multicultural or Multinational

Discussions over whether Canada is multinational or multicultural are numerous. The answer may be that it is both. Certainly most francophones in Quebec see themselves as a separate nationality, yet many of them also do not feel that is incompatible within a greater Canada. The same could be said of First Nations peoples. Those of British ancestry often have strong ties to the mother country, but not to the extent that they want to precisely copy it. They do not tend to like such things as titles of nobility, while former Foreign Affairs Minister John Manley even called for replacing the Crown with an elected head of state.

Adding to the complexity of all of this is the large influx of immigrants Canada has seen for more than a century. Most had no original identity with either France or Britain. They chose Canada out of a longing for economic opportunity, freedom, or both. Many have retained elements of their original cultures, but they hardly see themselves as any nationality other than Canadian.

These factors have created a society with a unique richness but not one without tensions. It is like having a home full of diverse and talented people trying to live together under one roof. Sometimes there are disagreements, but if they can get along the family seems to have someone who can do almost anything that may need to be done.

A Compassionate Society

Canada's Constitution calls for promoting equal opportunities for well being, furthering economic development for all, and providing essential public services for the entire nation. It also provides for equalization payments from Ottawa to the provinces to help reduce disparities in the level of services that any Canadians may receive. Today some see this approach to government as one of the critical elements in Canadian political culture that makes the country unique and also holds it together. It is something that English Canadians, French Canadians, and everyone else can uphold who shares this country's goal to be a compassionate society.

The idea is not without difficulty. Newfoundland and Nova Scotia claim that the federal government penalizes them for attempting to develop their oil and natural gas resources by reducing payments as provincial revenues from these industries increase. Alberta and Ontario are less than thrilled with helping to pay for equalization payments rather than receiving them. Still, there are very few calls for doing away with the system entirely. Until the late 1990s British Columbia also financially supported payments to other provinces. In the past so has Saskatchewan. With their current economic situations both are now recipients. Equalization payments have the flexibility to lessen the shock of temporary regional economic problems as well as chronic long-term ones.

Canada's healthcare system is another way in which the country seeks to reach out to everyone and try to prevent the unfortunate from falling through the cracks. Administered by the provinces and territories, and funded by both the provincial and federal governments, it is open to all citizens. Benefits do vary somewhat from province to province, so there is regional decision making in how the plan will function. Canadians pay taxes for this plan. Most feel it is worth it, and they are spared health insurance premiums as a result. A June 2001 survey by Leger Marketing indicated that a majority of Canadians were satisfied with the healthcare they receive. In a 2002 survey participants ranked the healthcare plan as the nation's greatest accomplishment in the twentieth century, with the Canadian Charter of Rights and Freedoms second.

The system is not perfect. Budget cutting at both the provincial and federal levels has led to cries of deteriorating service. Some provinces undoubtedly do provide a better level of care than others, and satisfaction in these regions appears to be higher than elsewhere. Stories are told of wealthier Canadians seeking treatment in the United States where they may have less waiting time for some services and find certain ones available that are not at home. Almost a third of the respondents in the Leger survey favored privatizing some, but not all, hospitals. The federal government has discussed the possibility of user fees to help ease the funding burden. While all of this may be the case, the Canadian plan does deliver, and most of the time it does it well. No person need fear being left out because he or she is unemployed or self-employed. Some Americans have gone so far as to propose at least parts of the plan as worthy of consideration by the United States.

Canadians and Americans both agree on the value of education. Debates over which nation does it better are probably pretty pointless, as both do it well. Most, but not all, Canadian universities are public rather than private institutions. As a result they are very affordable by American standards. Canadian students have long been attracted in considerable numbers to American educational institutions, but now, given the cost factor, more Americans are heading north of the border. The so-called

Canadian Ivy schools, such as the University of Toronto and Queens, in Kingston, Ontario, provide a superior education, at a very reasonable cost. Some Canadian universities that never did so until recent years are now recruiting American students, especially in states such as Florida, Texas, and California. In the area of education Canadian society again appears to create an environment that reflects the values of the country.

A Fragile Whole

There has been much talk in Canada and also in the United States about the possible disintegration of the Canadian state. That it is a possibility should not be ignored, but then how many Americans outside the state of Alaska realize that it has a political party which seriously advocates independence and that the state government once spent nearly a half million dollars of taxpayers' money to study the feasibility of secession? Scotland and Wales both have political parties that want to separate from London, and the stories of the breakup of the Soviet Union, Czechoslovakia, and Yugoslavia, now seem like ancient history. In short, Canada is far from being alone in facing this sort of problem. The challenge of maintaining a multinational state is an extremely difficult one.

Ironically some of the strength of Canadian nationhood has been overlooked by not examining carefully enough what most separatists in Quebec have been working to achieve. Former Quebec Premier, and one of the founders of the separatist Parti Quebecois, Rene Levesque referred to it as sovereignty-association. Not all separatists would agree on exactly what it would include, but generally it would seem to provide Quebec with complete control over its political affairs, yet closely link it with Canada. This would include a common customs union and currency at the very least. Other elements often mentioned are freedom of passage and immigration to and from Quebec and Canada, along with possibly a common citizenship. A consultative parliament for the two states, with a common defense force, is sometimes also suggested. One minister in a past Parti Quebecois government described it as an arrangement similar to the European Union. Sovereignist hard-liner Premier Bernard Landry took a similar approach in a July 2001 speech delivered in Belgium, where he was actually hailed as a federalist for his remarks!

Some anglophones feel this is a case of desiring to have your cake and eat it too. Perhaps in some ways it is, but sovereignty-association suggests that even those most unhappy with the Canadian Confederation find things about it that are of considerable value. If that is the case, then surely the rest of the country must find much in which they take pride. Perhaps it is the traditional Canadian reserve and modesty that makes them slower to declare their country's virtues than Americans are when talking about theirs. Yet even in Montreal on July 1, 2001, Canada Day, so many Maple Leaf flags were waving that the media took notice.

In the West there are also rumblings. Alberta has its Separation party, but the vast majority of Westerners want changes, not separation. First Nations clamor for protection of traditional hunting, fishing, and land rights, not for independence. The Cree Nation in particular has put forth a very careful legal presentation of the fact that it is part of Canada and does not desire to be a part of an independent Quebec.

During the 1960s America faced the turmoil brought by the Civil Rights movement. The Voting Rights Act and the Watts riots in Los Angeles seemed to reveal a nation at odds with itself. What was often not realized is that most of the angry were fighting to come fully into the American nation, not for the right to leave it. One should not compare Canada in this regard with the United States, but there are similarities. Canada is not the great melting pot that America has been. French Canadians in particular wish to retain their identity. Yet, there seems to be enough common ground among most of these peoples, enough that they all value and cherish, to say there truly is a Canadian.

AN ABUNDANCE OF RICHES
The Diverse Canadian Economy

To truly know a nation you need to know how its people earn their living, what they have to offer to each other, and what they are able to market to the world. Canada's natural resource wealth has long been recognized, but her economy has over the years developed a rich diversity, that is often not recognized. Commodities continue to play an important role, but so do many other things as well. In addition Canada can boast of some world-class companies in a number of areas of her economy, as well as more modest firms. As we explore Canada from a financial viewpoint, we will note some of these. They are included strictly for purposes of illustration. Nothing that follows is intended to offer investment suggestions of any kind. For those who wish to explore more deeply into Canadian financial markets, a special appendix of appropriate web sites is included. Numerous Canadian corporations also have their own pages on the Internet.

Let us now begin by looking at Canadian financial markets and the differences and similarities they have with those in the United States. It is appropriate that we begin with an old established sector of Canada's economic activity.

The Grain Market

Canadian grain trading is big business and is handled on the Winnipeg Commodity Exchange (WCE). Markets are maintained for barley, feed wheat, canola, field peas, oats, and flaxseed. In the past the Commodity Exchange has also done business in nonagricultural products such as precious metals. It offers both futures and options, but both are not available for some commodities. These trading instruments permit agricultural producers to lock in a price today for a crop that will be harvested at a later date. In the hands of professionals, they can help stabilize prices and make markets function more efficiently.

One of Canada's major grain ports is Thunder Bay, Ontario, on the north shore of Lake Superior. From here wheat can be shipped through the Great Lakes and the Saint Lawrence Seaway to Europe and other destinations throughout the world. Vancouver, along with Prince Rupert, British Columbia, serves a similar purpose for Pacific Rim exports, while a modest amount of grain for the European market is shipped by rail to the northern Manitoba port of Churchill on the west coast of Hudson Bay.

Canadian wheat and barley sales are for the most part handled in a fashion that probably seems strange to Americans and has not been without some controversy in Canada itself. In 1935, during the Great Depression, in order to support and assist the distressed grain farmers, Ottawa set up the Canadian Wheat Board as a Crown or government corporation (somewhat similar to the Tennessee Valley Authority in the United States). While trading of wheat futures is permitted, the Wheat Board handles all actual sales and exports of Western (but not elsewhere) wheat and barley, which is 95 percent of the Canadian crop. The idea behind the approach is that by granting the Wheat Board this kind of authority it can negotiate better prices for the producers. Neither the Wheat Board nor the Canadian government subsidizes grain growers. Its employees are not civil servants but paid by the farmers they serve. Canada does not restrict the volume of American wheat imports into the country, and all American grains enter duty-free.

Generally Canadian prairie grain farmers have been satisfied with the operation of the Wheat Board, supply it with grain, and help to govern it. In recent years some have felt they could do better on their own, and a few have illegally attempted to do so. There have been calls for changes in the Wheat Board and even for its outright demise, but for the immediate future, at least, it probably will continue to handle sales of these two important grain commodities for Western farmers.

The Wheat Board works with private companies in the marketing and exporting of grain. In some cases this involves another Canadian concept, the grain pool, such as Saskatchewan Wheat Pool or Manitoba-based Agricore-United, which was created in 2001 by the merger of United Grain Growers, Limited, and Agricore Co-operative, Limited. Farmers voluntarily belong to the pools, which can store their wheat, market it to the Wheat Board, and then assist the Board in exporting it out of the country. Pools also are involved in other unregulated agricultural enterprises.

Before leaving the subject of Canadian agriculture, we might briefly mention a few other crops grown across this vast nation. Quebec farmers produce vegetables, soybeans, wheat, and corn. Vegetables are also important in Ontario, while grapes are one of the major commodities of the southern part of that province. Since the passage of the Milk Act in1960, Ontario's dairy farmers have sold their products through an arrangement somewhat similar to the Wheat Board. Today Dairy Farmers of Ontario is the organization responsible for all marketing activities under the appropriate provincial legislation. Dairy farming comprises the largest segment of Ontario agriculture and accounts for approximately 20 percent of the total.

Blueberries are plentiful in Nova Scotia, and one of the country's best-known crops is the Prince Edward Island potato, which is promoted by the Potato Board. Unlike the Wheat Board, the Potato Board is not directly involved in the sale of the commodity but rather acts as an advisor and supporter to the growers and marketers. Clearly, Canadian agriculture is varied and plays a vital role in the nation's economy.

The Stock Exchanges

Canada has no national equivalent of the Security and Exchange Commission in the United States. Instead, financial exchanges are regulated at the provincial level. As a result, the quality and nature of regulation varies from province to province. Proposals for some sort of national regulatory system have been made, but so far none has generated the necessary support to become a reality. Understandably, provincial governments are reluctant to give up the authority they currently possess. While the present system for the most part works satisfactorily, there may be future calls for a more integrated national approach.

In late 1999 and early 2000 Canadian stock exchanges underwent a major reorganization that had been proposed several months earlier. The result has been a closer working relationship among all of them as well as an arrangement that increasingly resembles something like a national stock market. The Toronto Stock Exchange (TSE) continues to be the biggest, as it has been for many years. Essentially all large and mid-size Canadian companies whose shares are traded publicly will be listed here.

Two Western exchanges, the Vancouver Stock Exchange and the Calgary-based Alberta Stock Exchange came together to form the Canadian Venture Exchange. Shortly later the small Winnipeg Stock Exchange agreed to transfer its listings to the Venture Exchange. With headquarters in Calgary, trading takes place both there and in Vancouver, a situation not unlike the former Pacific Stock Exchange, which traded in both San Francisco and Los Angeles. Junior or small companies, many of which may be relatively new, are the specialty of the Venture Exchange. Companies that start here may automatically graduate to the Toronto Exchange once they achieve the necessary size and maturity.

The Venture Exchange appears to have made considerable success in improving the image of its two parent exchanges. While the vast majority of listings on both were fine, and some turned out to be outstanding investments, unfortunately a few "bad apples" occasionally turned up, usually in the form of oil companies with much enthusiasm but more cow pasture than petroleum, in the case of Alberta, and concept companies long on dreams but short on products or sales, in Vancouver, plus a few outright deliberate frauds. The Venture Exchange has tightened listing standards and more closely watched the companies it has accepted. Toronto, whose standards have generally been high, has had a few embarrassments of its own, including Bre-X Minerals, whose Indonesian gold mine turned out to be fraudulent. It also is intent to prevent future occurrences of this nature.

In 2001 the Venture Exchange agreed to be acquired by the Toronto Stock Exchange, and today is known as the TSX Venture Exchange. The two exchanges continue to operate as separate entities, in a manner similar to the American Stock Exchange and the Nasdaq after their merger.

While some stock index futures and options for the Toronto Stock Exchange trade on the Toronto Futures Exchange, the vast majority of options, futures, and other derivative financial products now trade on the Montreal Stock Exchange, or the Bourse de Montreal. The Exchange also refers to itself as the Canadian Derivatives Exchange. Actually Montreal is the country's oldest stock market and until the reorganization of the stock markets listed a number of major Canadian companies, sometimes duplicating Toronto. While these have now been transferred to Toronto, Montreal continues to maintain listings and regulatory services for a number of junior or small-capitalization Quebec-based companies, while using TSX Venture facilities for actual trading in these shares.

In the United States thousands of companies whose stock is publicly traded are not listed on any stock exchange or the regular Nasdaq network. These are the so-called over-the-counter stocks, and dealers interested in buying and selling them can make their own offers. Canada also has an over-the-counter market for numerous companies. Many Canadian corporations also list their stock on exchanges in the United States.

The Companies

A tour of Canadian companies that represent the various areas of its multifaceted economy, may reveal many names that are new, but at least several might be familiar. Some of these businesses operate in the United

States and in other countries throughout the world. Let us take a look at the variety the country has to offer.

Service Companies: A *Forbes*, August 7, 2000, report noted that it is not the traditional timber and mining operations but rather the service sector that has seen the most growth in the Canadian economy in recent years. The report went on to indicate that growth has been particularly good in communications, business services, and wholesale trade. When you begin to explore these areas, a number of impressive corporations come into view. An example is The Thomson Corporation, a publisher, and one of Canada's largest companies. In recent years it has been moving rapidly and heavily into the electronic aspects of this business. Another impressive publisher and media company is Quebecor. In the field of cellular and digital communications, along with cable, and radio and television operations, Rogers Communications stands out as a major player.

A giant in the Canadian economy and the communications sector is of course BCE . The parent company's largest holding is Bell Canada, the dominant telephone company in both Ontario and Quebec. Along with BCE subsidiaries, it really has a significant presence throughout the country. One such subsidiary is Aliant . The company was the result of the merger of four telephone companies in Atlantic Canada, and has done rather well in an area of the country which has not prospered as much as some other regions. BCE and Aliant have now been reorganized into trust arrangements that should result in larger dividend payments to their shareholders.

In the transportation area the privatized former government carrier Air Canada is a dominant figure. Its acquisition of struggling Canadian Airlines as a subsidiary in 2000 might strengthen the entire airline situation in the country and will create a network that with regional partners serves virtually all of it. Air Canada, like the airline industry in general, experienced the damage of the September 11 World Trade Center tragedy. Challenging skies may lie ahead for quite some time. Nevertheless, this is the country's most important air carrier. Although it had to seek bankruptcy protection, it may ultimately have a brighter future.

Both Canadian National Railway and Canadian Pacific Railway Company are major North American rail carriers. Canadian National has continued to be successful since its denationalization. Canadian Pacific Railway has always been a publicly owned company and until recently was part of Canadian Pacific Limited, which operated a variety of businesses. In 2001 this venerable, old Canadian financial organization decided to break up into five different companies. The other four are Fairmont Hotels and Resorts, which operates some of the best and most famous hotels in the country, the former Pan Canadian Energy Corporation, now part of EnCana, a major North American petroleum producer, marine shipper CP Ships Limited, and Fording, Inc., which mines coal in southern British Columbia and Alberta. In 2003 Fording entered into a partnership with several other companies to create the Fording Canadian Coal Trust.

The financial sector offers plenty of significant enterprises. Major Banks include Royal Bank of Canada, Canadian Imperial Bank of Commerce, commonly referred to as CIBC, Bank of Montreal and Bank of Nova Scotia, or ScotiaBank, as it is better known. Insurance listings include life and health insurer Great-West Lifeco, a holding company whose life and health insurance subsidiary headquartered in Winnipeg, does considerable business in the United States as well as Canada. Another company in the life and health insurance fields is Sun Life Financial Services of Canada.

Technology: In addition to the almost universally known Nortel Networks, Canada is home to a number of other technology companies. Cognicase refers to itself as an "e-business integrator and Wireless/ Internet electronic solutions provider." DataMirror Corporation is a provider of software and processing, specializing in "Interconnected data solutions." C-MAC Industries, headquartered in Montreal, was a major "designer and manufacturer of integrated electronic manufacturing solutions." Solectron, its American competitor in the past, has now acquired the company.

Still other technology companies would include British Columbia-based Sierra Wireless, a producer of wireless communications equipment. Celestica Inc. provides electronic manufacturing services to original equipment manufacturers primarily in the computer and communications fields. JDS Uniphase actually can be considered a joint Canadian-American corporation with headquarters both in San Jose, California, and Nepean, a suburb of Ottawa, Ontario. The company provides advanced fiber optic components and modules. Its customers are telecommunications and cable television companies. Research in Motion is a Canadian mid-capitalization company dealing with wireless communications technology and sells the highly popular BlackBerry. Canada's telecommunications and technology companies received no exemption from the destruction of the stock-market crash that several years ago hit the technology and telecommunications sectors, but many of these are now thriving once again, and this segment of the country's economy should have the strength to prosper in the future.

Natural Resources: The natural resources sector is one with which Canada has long been associated. That association is quite understandable given the fact that this sector still makes important contributions to the nation's economy. Barrick Gold has a reputation for being one of the most efficient producers of the precious metal anywhere. Its acquisition of American-based Homestake mining makes it an even more dominant producer and gives it substantial opportunities in Australia as well. Few companies in the United States or Canada can boast of significant production of either platinum or palladium. One that does well with both is North American Palladium. Inco, Limited is well known as a nickel producer but also mines copper, precious metals, and cobalt. The company has been so attractive that on October 24, 2006, the Brazilian mining corporation Companhia Vale de Rio Doce acquired ownership. Potash Corporation of Saskatchewan produces nitrogen, phosphate, and potash for fertilizer. A more speculative operation is Aber Diamond Limited. This company owns 40 percent of the Diavik Diamond Project at Lac de Gras, north of Yellowknife in the Northwest Territories.

In the energy sector BC Gas Inc., is a gas distributor and transmitter as well as an oil pipeline operator. Alberta Energy Corporation was a major company in both oil and gas exploration and production. In January 2002 Alberta Energy and previously-mentioned Pan Canadian Energy announced plans to merge and form a new company known as EnCana. This corporation is a significant petroleum and gas producer in the world market with projects in Alberta, British Columbia, the United States, additional areas of Canada, and the North Sea. Other major petroleum and gas producers, all with headquarters in Calgary, include Talisman Energy, Canadian Natural Resources, Paramount Resources, Canex Energy, and Husky Energy. Some of these companies have extensive operations outside Canada as well as in their own country. An October 30, 2006 *Barron's* article reported extensively on Canadian Natural Resources promising Horizon Project that is seeking to extract oil from the sands of northern Alberta. TransCanada Pipelines, as its name suggests, is a natural gas transmitter rather than a gas producer. In addition the company is a power producer. Canada's energy companies now supply more hydrocarbons to the United States than come from any other country.

The traditional forest products sector remains well represented. Canada's largest timber company is British Columbia's Canfor Corporation. TimberWest Forest Corporation is a forest products company with headquarters in Vancouver. Another British Columbia company, Taiga Forest Products is a distributor of lumber, panel board, and other building products. Still another British Columbia producer is Doman Industries Limited, while Tembec Incorporated, has its headquarters in Quebec with lumber operations throughout Canada. At times the Canadian timber industry has suffered severe pressure from American tariffs that the producers feel are unwarranted, and which American homebuilders dislike.

Other Companies: There are a number of Canadian subsidiaries of large, well known American companies. General Motors' Canadian company is based in Oshawa, Ontario. Sears Canada is of course an important retailer.

Names of some retail outlets have long been associated with Canada. Hudson's Bay Company, as we previously noted, is the oldest continuously existing corporation in the world. It operates stores under its Bay and other names in major Canadian cities. The northern outposts the Hudson's Bay Company was famous for serving in the past are now

Northern Stores run by the North West Company Fund. They provide everything from groceries to clothing and appliances. The North West Company also serves Alaska.

A company that seems to be involved in almost everything is Onex Corporation. It has electronics manufacturing services, but also does airline catering, outsourced marketing services, and even sugar refining. Bombardier is another Canadian company that increasingly has an international reputation. It is a serious competitor with Boeing and Airbus in aerospace design and manufacturing and is a world-class producer of rail equipment, including subway cars. Finally, we might mention the well-known Alcan Inc., which is a multinational aluminum and packaging company.

This is hardly an exhaustive list. It does not even attempt to explore the many small capitalization companies you will find listed on the web sites of the TSX Venture and Montreal Exchanges. However, it is a starting point. Hopefully it has helped to demonstrate just how rich and varied the Canadian economy has become. Some parts of the country offer more economic activity and variety than others, but every region has something to offer.

The State of the Canadian Economy

Perhaps we have saved the most important matter for last. What sort of future is in store for the Canadian economy? While the patterns of recent years have not yet indicated such a move, the growing importance of the European Union, NAFTA, and the Pacific Rim, could in the future help Canada diversify its export markets and become less dependent on the United States. Also, because natural resources continue to play a prominent, if not quite so dominant, role in the Canadian economy, the nation's markets may in periods of inflation do better than those of many other countries, including the United States.

One advantage Canada, along with Western Europe, does have over some international markets is its political stability. There need be no concern of violent revolution or other similar political upheaval. That naturally raises the question of Quebec. Although the Liberal party's victory in the 2003 provincial election has for now reduced concerns about the matter, should Quebec at some future date decide to leave Canada, there is no reason to believe that separation would be any more violent than that between the Czech Republic and Slovakia. It is extremely difficult to imagine Canadians as a whole using violence on each other for political purposes. Also, as we have already seen, the result is more likely to be a legal separation rather than an actual divorce. Sovereignty-association would leave in place some strong economic links and possibly some modest political ones as well. Any injury to the Canadian economy would probably be temporary.

There are some signs that point to strength in the Canadian economy. For one thing, the country was able to avoid much of the dot.com mania that created painful financial excesses in American markets, especially the Nasdaq. A July 9, 2001, *Barron's* editorial did note the difficulty that Canadian companies experience when seeking to raise venture capital for new economic enterprises, and that government regulation is sometimes the culprit. Despite this, the amount of money available is growing, while the gap between what Canadian companies can raise compared to their American counterparts is shrinking. *Barron's* in a July 2, 2001, article projected better earnings growth and a lower price/earnings ratio in 2002 for Canada than for either the United States or most of Western Europe. The prediction turned out to be correct, with the Canadian budget remaining balanced, and in 2003 the Canadian dollar strengthening. It strengthened further in 2004 and 2005. Under Prime Minister Paul Martin the federal government continued to maintain a balanced budget with modest surpluses. In the years ahead Canada should do well, but no one can make precise predictions too far into the future. Asia could possibly do better, but risk and volatility are certainly much higher there.

A typical example of the strength and diversity of Canada's economy was its April 2001 report in which it recorded a strong trade surplus of 6.33 billion Canadian dollars, coming from strong shipments of automobiles and parts, energy, and timber. Obviously an excessive surplus can create problems, as Japan has discovered, but Canada appears to show healthy signs of promoting its products while not importing more than it can afford. Meanwhile the country enjoys a higher savings rate than does the United States. If the rate of taxation is higher, those taxes reduce or eliminate other costs such as health insurance premiums and some educational expenses.

Certainly all is not perfect. During the 1990s income growth for Canadian families was essentially stagnant, while Americans enjoyed solid gains. Probably the chief reason why Canada did not fare so well was that both the federal and provincial governments were in the process of putting their financial houses in order and were less generous with some benefits than previously. By the end of the decade Canadians were starting to see some improvement over what the income situation had been several years earlier. Also, by the summer of 2001 the Canadian economy was generating a higher percentage of new jobs than was that of the United States.

Despite some good news, Canada did not escape the economic downturn of 2001 and 2002. The Canadian economy experienced the same kinds of difficulty nearly all developed countries were facing. Downsizing in certain industries continued, some American-based companies closed Canadian plants, and the Canadian dollar sank to a new low against the American dollar before later reversing course and achieving its best highs in many years during 2005 and 2006. Provincial and federal governments found budgeting, and avoiding future deficits, much more difficult, but for the most part were able to stay the course. The economy, like that of the United States, was in a recession, and the Bank of Canada lowered interest rates in an attempt to stem the tide.

Some regional problems emerged as well. A severe summer drought crippled parts of the Western grain belt, the last coal mine closed on Cape Breton Island, Nova Scotia, and the timber industry suffered from an American-imposed tariff, which Canada felt was unjustified under current trade agreements. Obviously Canada is not an economic utopia immune from the business cycles and other problems that advanced economies encounter. On the other hand, just as the United States emerged from the downturn of 2001-2002, so did Canada, and it began to put down a foundation for a still stronger economic future. As we have seen, by 2003 the currency reversed its fall, and interest rates had also risen. By 2003 Canada was the only G-7 still reporting a budget surplus. An upsurge in commodities prices, dramatically visible by 2004, has done much to strengthen her economy and financial markets. Her increasingly diverse economy and the other strengths we have seen she possesses should mean a bright future lies ahead.

Maybe an indication of what can happen and a prediction of what is to come was a highly successful trade tour to Winnipeg and Toronto in July 2001 by colorful Minnesota Governor Jesse Ventura. Ventura charmed and entertained his enthusiastic audiences, but his purpose was really to get down to serious business. He was aware that Minnesota exports of electronic equipment to Canada in 2000 were over one billion dollars and that Canadian trade with his state exceeds that of Britain, Japan, and China combined. The former Governor of Minnesota seemed confident he could generate more of a good thing. Minnesota was also. It planned to have Ventura engage in more such activity after his term in office expired.

Indeed there are good things for both countries. It is no secret that American investment in Canada is extensive. What may be less known is that by the end of 1999 Canada had $80 billion invested in the United States, an increase of almost $6 billion over 1998. Only four countries had more.

No one can precisely predict the economic and political future of Canada, or any other nation for that matter. What can be said with certainty is this is a nation with a strong, multifaceted economy, and richly endowed with natural resources. She also possesses a well-educated multicultural work force and a world-class infrastructure. As a result the future economic story of Canada may be a very attractive one

PERSONAL EXPLORATIONS
Travel to and in Canada

The Legal Stuff

By now are you at least a little curious? Do you want a pleasant holiday, and one that need not break the budget, unless you just feel like over indulging a little? Then why not consider a Canadian exploration of your own? It should be informative, relaxing, enjoyable, and quite possibly filled with some unexpected but pleasant discoveries. The requirements for entry into Canada and a smooth return home are rather basic, but it helps to know what they are before you make the trip and thus reduce the possibility of unanticipated surprises and delays.

Until recently Americans did not need a passport to visit Canada as a tourist, but now they do. In any case, a passport speeds up immigration and customs matters and makes it possible to exchange currency. Your passport is the necessary proof of your American citizenship. If working, studying, or planning an extended stay, an inquiry with Canadian Immigration is highly recommended in order to make sure you meet all entry requirements.

Canada will not admit convicted felons, or persons who pose a security or health threat. Visitors must also have sufficient funds to cover their expenses while in the country. Laws on firearms are strict. Sporting rifles and shotguns may be imported, but only if declared to Canada Customs when first entering the country. Under no circumstances attempt to bring in handguns, any kind of semi or fully automatic weapons, or any undeclared firearms of any kind. To attempt to do so will result in criminal charges.

Your driver's license is good throughout Canada. Check to be sure, but your automobile and health insurance policies should also cover you. Ask your insurance agent or company for a card that identifies your carrier and gives evidence that you meet the minimum liability insurance requirements in all provinces and territories. This is free.

Many Canadian businesses, especially those accustomed to dealing with tourists, will accept American currency. They are never required to do so, and you sometimes get a poor exchange rate. It is not difficult to get a small amount of Canadian currency before you leave either from your bank or American Express, if you are a cardholder. Your AAA office, travel agent, or bank may sell travelers' checks denominated in Canadian dollars, but be sure to use these before returning home to avoid the cost of exchanging them back into American dollars. Most Canadian banks will readily exchange American dollar travelers' checks with proper identification, such as a passport. Always check, but your ATM cards are probably acceptable as well as your calling cards and cellular phone. Make sure you understand whatever fees or additional charges may be required for their use. For regular purchases, Visa, Mastercard, and American Express are widely accepted throughout Canada.

It certainly is not a requirement, but if you plan to visit any predominantly French-speaking areas, especially Quebec, consider buying a small phrase book and learning just a few words of French. A friendly *"bonjour"* or *"merci"* requires no effort and will often delight your hosts. If you show an acceptance of their language, they are much happier speaking yours.

For more detailed information on traveling in Canada you can go to the Government of Canada's general web site (http://www.gc.ca/). This will provide access to immigration services and can also direct you to various provincial and territorial sources for general travel information.

Any search engine will also list a variety of Canadian travel information sites, both government and private. The AAA has very useful TourBooks for Canada that are free to members. Any bookstore should offer a selection of travel guides. Two of my personal favorites are those by Fodor's and Baedeker.

Eventually we all need to return home. There are a few things to keep in mind when clearing American customs. If you are flying back to the United States, in many cases you will go through American customs in the airport before you leave Canada. Do not pack items or papers you may have to show where they cannot be readily retrieved if required by the customs officials. If you have been out of the United States at least forty-eight hours, and not used your exemption in the last thirty days, you are entitled to bring back up to $800 duty free. A husband and wife may combine their exemptions, regardless of how much either purchased, into a total of $1600. There is a limit of one liter of alcohol, 200 cigarettes, and 100 cigars per person. You may bring back more alcohol or tobacco, but duty will be assessed, and large quantities may arouse the curiosity of customs personnel.

Tobacco and any other products produced in Cuba or brought into Canada from Cuba are prohibited and will be confiscated, even though they were purchased legally in Canada. Goods from other countries with whom Americans are barred from trading are also not permitted entry. You can get further details on all possible restrictions by going to the United States Customs web site (http://www.customs.ustreas.gov/). Here you can also read and print the helpful little brochure *Know Before You Go,* which will answer nearly all the questions most tourists are likely to ask.

The first $1000 of declared goods in excess of your personal exemption is taxed at a favorable rate, currently no more than 10 percent. In addition, because of the NAFTA treaty, items that are produced in either Canada or Mexico may now enter the United States completely duty-free or at a very low rate. There is never a tariff on books or similar printed matter. In reality most tourists should be able to "shop till they drop" in Canada with very little fear of being presented a big bill by United States Customs.

There is one other "taxing matter" that needs attention. This is Canada's federal GST, General Tax on Goods and Services. It is essentially a 6 percent national sales tax. In addition, all provinces, except Alberta (and the territories), levy a sales tax, and these tend to be higher than what Americans are used to paying at home. Newfoundland, Nova Scotia, and New Brunswick have permitted their former provincial taxes to be merged with the federal one, and a Harmonized Sales Tax, currently 14 percent, is collected. Keep the taxes in mind when making purchases.

Canada used to refund the GST and the Harmonized Tax to visitors. Unfortunately since April 1, 2007, this is no longer the case. There is of course always the possibility that in the future the policy may change again. If you want to check on the present status of the GST you can go to the web site of the Canada Revenue Agency at

(http://www.cra-arc.gc.ca). Ontario will refund the provincial sales tax on goods but not accommodations, and only if you spend at least $625. Each receipt must total at least $50 in Canadian currency. The other provinces do not offer refunds, although some did in the past. Ontario sales tax information and forms are available at (http://www.rev.gov.on.ca/ images/rsie0298.pdf). You can also call (905) 432-3332. Check on the current requirements before you go to make sure your receipts have all required information and whether you may need documentation from Canadian Customs that the goods have been taken out of the country.

Now that we have all this legal stuff out of the way, it is time for things more interesting. Please do not consider the adventures below any kind of suggested tour itinerary or even areas that you should visit. For most travelers some of them would hardly make their "must-see" list. They are places I have visited in Canada, and all of them have for some reason made this splendid country a very special one for me. They are presented here with the hope that you will indeed find them entertaining. Yet they are intended for more than that. Possibly one or two of them may stir your soul to seek out your own special Canadian treasures, those spots that will speak to your very depths in a personal way, calling you to what is really important. So explore a portion of my journey. Permit it to be a door to opening up one of your own. Let us begin.

Thank You TWA

Somewhere out there a former Trans World Airlines pilot does not realize it, but he deserves my deepest thanks. He gave me wings that for just a few moments, but long enough, enabled me to have an encounter with one of my mystical places. Sable Island is a crescent-shaped spit of land that lies approximately 100 miles eastward from the mainland of Nova Scotia, the province of which it technically is a part. Rightfully called a "Graveyard of the Atlantic," it has been claiming vessels at least since 1583, when the explorer who took possession of Newfoundland for England, Sir Humphrey Gilbert, lost one of his three ships there. Colonists from several European countries tried to establish settlements, but all eventually failed. Later it would be home to lighthouse keepers and life savers whose job was to furnish assistance to distressed mariners who ran aground. Sable Island never seems to offer comfort to any who seek to tame her.

Perhaps in some ways her wild life has best understood the island's ways and tended to thrive, unless destroyed by humans. The most famous are the wild horses, probably better known as the Sable Island Ponies. Introduced around the mid-eighteenth century, the horses are still there, a kind of symbol of the boundless, untamed, freedom that is Sable Island. They have not been without controversy, some claiming they destroy the natural environment, while others just as strongly say they maintain it. The animals have been exploited, the better ones having been shipped from time to time to the mainland and sold. They have been victimized by well-meaning attempts to save or improve them, and may ultimately be seen as incompatible with the economic boom that is now taking place in the waters around Sable Island. Despite all this, they continue to roam this remote, haunting land they have made their own.

Cattle actually came to the island two hundred years earlier than the horses, and for a time did well until driven into extinction, although some of their descendants survive on the mainland. Foxes, also no longer here, were probably the first mammals on Sable, and it has been a home to seals, the walrus, and other creatures. Birds have thrived, and terns continue to call this home.

Over the years, Sable remained a more or less quiet, forgotten place. The last shipwreck was 1947, and all attempts up to that time to promote commercial development had pretty much ended in failure. Things might have remained that way. It was not to be. In 1959 a permit was granted for oil drilling. In 1971 the oilmen finally hit pay dirt. A successful well was drilled. There is oil on and around Sable Island, but the really big finds were the natural gas deposits off shore discovered somewhat later. By the late 1990s Nova Scotia was starting to think of the gas as one of the keys to the province's future economy.

So, Sable Island no longer is a forgotten graveyard. In fact in one way it is no longer even an island, as a gas pipeline now links it to the rest of Nova Scotia. In time it will probably cease to be the place I saw briefly but will remember always.

We boarded the Trans World Airlines flight in Rome for the trip to New York. The flight attendants went through the usual greeting procedure, and I noticed while seeking my seat the route map posted on the wall of the cabin. I made some comment about it looked as if we might fly somewhere near Sable Island and that I had spotted it once out the window of an airplane but at a distance so far away it was little more than a dot in the ocean. More to myself than anyone I remarked it would be intriguing to go to such a remote place.

The flight was pleasant enough with the usual airplane food and in-flight movies, neither one of which, on this or any other carrier, was likely to make the journey memorable. We were well on our way toward New York when the captain came on the public address system. He asked those sitting on the left side of the airplane (my side) to please look out the windows, as we were about to make a close pass by Sable Island. Indeed we did. It was almost directly below, its beautiful crescent shape, distinct and unforgettable, surrounded by the waters of the North Atlantic. Of course the altitude was too great for any surface details, but not so great as to shut off the imagination. I think I could hear the sounds of hoofs on the dunes, during those few brief moments it took to pass by this island that had become for now my private preserve. All too soon it was but a memory. The landing at Kennedy Airport would have been uneventful except for one matter. As I left the plane I was presented the flight map.

It had been no accident we toured Sable Island that day. Thank you TWA. Thanks for the memories.

If you would like to discover more about Sable Island and possibly assist with its preservation, visit the web site of the Sable Island Preservation Trust (http://www.sabletrust.ns.ca/). This is a nonprofit organization seeking to preserve a place that deserves to be preserved while recognizing that commercial energy development here is inevitable.

Sheshatsheits: Looking for the Key

We reached Goose Bay several hours before our scheduled landing. The ferry office was closed at this early morning hour, and the small port area was about two miles from town. No telephones were available. The only thing to do was make the uphill journey on foot, as I was alone and without any vehicle. Believe it or not, Labrador in June, even early in the morning, can be warm, maybe hot. In addition one soon becomes aware of something else for which it is known at this time of the year, namely rather aggressive flies. W. C. Fields' immortal line about "rather being in Philadelphia," seemed most appropriate at this moment. I continued on, in the semi-isolation, gradually becoming warmer and more uncomfortable as I slowly made progress toward my destination.

Then it happened. Perhaps it was a gift from heaven. I really did not know or care. Down that road, believe it or not, came a genuine taxicab. Have you ever thought about attempting to hail a taxi in the middle of Labrador? If you really want one, do not think about it. Just do it. Hesitate, and it may be too late, forever. Well, at least it seemed that way. I did not hesitate, and hailed that cab. The driver was as surprised as I was. He had been hoping for a possible fare at the port, but quickly accepted my offer to hire him as tour guide, a position that he readily admitted he had never held before. A strange pair, off we went, touring Labrador by taxi.

My guide, who had lived in nearby North West River all his life, except for a brief time in St. John's, Newfoundland, in order to go to school, turned out to be quite skilled at his new profession. Before our journey together was done, he would make able use of the one paved highway in the area, Provincial Highway 520, to show me the highlights of Happy Valley-Goose Bay, two towns that had merged into one, along with his own community of North West River. The Goose, as it is commonly known, is dominated by its NATO military base, used primarily for low-level flight training, and at the time manned mostly by Germans. It also has the only hospital in the area, a few hotels, a couple of small museums, and a modest civilian airport. There are commercial timber operations in the area, as one can tell from spotting lumber near the dock, stacked, waiting, ready to be shipped. If not a rival to Toronto or Montreal, it does at least offer the necessary amenities of life. Adjacent Happy Valley is the location of the city hall and also provides a nice vantage point to view the Churchill, or, as it was originally called, Grand River. The river can take you to the nearby small community of Mud Lake, accessible only by boat, and on into the interior to the hydroelectric project at Churchill Falls and part of the way to the iron-mining towns of Wabush and Labrador City. You can reach those settlements by taking the Trans-Labrador Highway, a gravel, unpaved road, without facilities, which begins at Goose Bay. It is open nearly all year, but spring floods may still close it for a few weeks. Improvements are intended to eliminate that problem.

On the other end of Provincial Highway 520, some thirty kilometers distant from Happy Valley, my guide showed me the sights of North West River. From Sunday Hill, an enjoyable place to sit or even picnic during a Labrador summer, there are magnificent views of Lake Melville, Grand Lake, and the Mealy Mountains. In town are a modest medical clinic, small branch of a college, and of course a Northern Store, where almost anything is available for purchase. An inviting, little, white church building is shared by the Anglican, United Church, and Moravian congregations. Most intriguing is an old abandoned Hudson's Bay Company building. In years past traders would come by boat and canoe to do business here. It has been given to the community, which had not yet decided what to do with it.

As fascinating as all this northern journey had been, it is not what I most remember, what has left the vivid picture in my mind. Across a small bridge from North West River is the town of Sheshatsheits. My driver took me there also. Sheshatsheits is primarily populated by Innu, a major

Indian band (tribe) in this region, and should not be confused with the Inuit (Eskimo), although there are a few of them, along with several white residents, there also. At one time it was part of North West River, but the Innu ultimately felt that they wanted control of their own affairs and decided to establish a separate government. Evidently there was no serious objection in North West River, and the two communities seem to get along quite well together. Out of sensitivity for the social problems that can sometimes plague native communities in the isolation of the North, North West River had remained dry. Thirsty residents of either place had to make the trip into Goose Bay for alcoholic beverages.

Unlike the paved streets of North West River, those of Sheshatsheits were rock or gravel. Groups of houses had a strange sameness about them, government-built, and all constructed in a particular year. A quiet absence of economic activity pervaded the town. There was no clinic or college. Only one store seemed visible, although there may have been others in the vicinity. You sensed that life here was far from easy. You can understand why the children of native peoples are sometimes deeply troubled, tempted by gasoline sniffing or even suicide. They need to find the key to a more hopeful future.

Yet here on the shore of Lake Melville, there were also signs of possibility and hope. The leadership of the Innu band was determined to make life better in the community. Unfortunately in the past money received in settlement of tribal claims was sometimes permitted to trickle away. This was no longer the case. Recent payments had financed a new water system, and now there was a facility for assistance to troubled children. The band also had a new headquarters building. If there were difficulties here there was also determination.

It would be easy to say to Innu and other First Nations youth, if you want to make progress you must leave your traditional settlements and reserves. Some probably will take that option. Yet, if First Nations cultures are allowed to wither totally away Canada is going to be much poorer as a result. There is as an intangible richness that can thrive only in these places and among these peoples, who after all were the first Canadians. The key must be found to enable their communities to thrive, and it will not be found in Ottawa or any other place, other than among the First Nations themselves. It is not a smooth path. At times it is very painful, but it is one that can be taken.

My Labrador taxi tour eventually ended. I said goodbye to my helpful guide at the ferry office, and went inside to handle the details for the return passage to Newfoundland. For some totally unknown reason, I had always wanted to telephone someone from Goose Bay, Labrador. Now was my chance. I called a friend in Florida. This was my once-in-a-lifetime opportunity to talk about Labrador weather and sites while "on location." There was also time to go across the street to a small restaurant, the only eating-place around. I opted for the caribou burger. I am aware of the vital role the caribou, or *tuktu*, plays in the survival of the Inuit and certain First Nations bands, but for the rest of us it may be an acquired taste.

St. Pierre et Miquelon: VOCM, Moose, and Al Capone

An eerie feeling came over me in those early morning hours as I made the journey down the Trans-Canada Highway from St. John's toward the little town of Fortune, Newfoundland. The fog was as thick as the proverbial pea soup, not an unusual event for a Newfoundland morning. Radio Station VOCM was attempting its best to reassure me as I continued. American radio stations always begin their call letters with either a "K" or a "W" in accord with an international agreement on such matters. Canadian stations appropriately enough use a "C." Just a very few stations located in Newfoundland began broadcasting before that former colony joined Canada in 1949. They were assigned calls starting with a "V," and were permitted to keep them after the merger. VOCM is quite popular in St. John's and has the largest audience of these old pre-Confederation rarities.

From Twillingate I received the morning iceberg report along with local poetry from the Twillingate iceberg reporter. You cannot get the iceberg report at home. I realized I was indeed in a very different land. Then the moose sightings followed, with the usual words of caution to motorists such as me. I continued gazing through the windshield. It was a most uncomfortable feeling to know the warnings were completely useless. In that soup you would never see the moose in time for you and the animal to avoid an unscheduled and unwanted meeting. Fortunately the moose in this part of the island must have decided to sleep in that morning.

Eventually I turned off the Trans-Canada and began the trek down the Burin Peninsula. The first part of the Burin is so barren and sparsely populated, I felt as if I were back in Labrador. Eventually civilization did reappear with the sighting of a McDonalds in Marystown. Then it was on to Grand Bank.

Grand Bank is still a rather neat, picturesque community. It once was a major center for the fishing industry, and a large processing plant remains in the harbor area. Today most of the boats, along with the plant, were idle, as the government had put severe limits on the size of the catch in the badly depleted fishery. Hopefully someday the boats will sail again, but for now the harbor was strangely quiet.

There was plenty of time to eat and explore the town. Its leading attraction is the provincially maintained Seamen's Museum. Since it was closed for the Newfoundland Discovery Day holiday in honor of John Cabot, I would actually have to wait until my return to visit the interior, but even an outside inspection proved rather fascinating. The building appropriately enough for a seaport has a roof line suggestive of sails on a schooner. It once housed the Yugoslav pavilion at the 1967 Expo World's Fair in Montreal. After the fair's closing the province bought it and shipped it here. The actual exhibits effectively tell the story of the courageous people who made their living from the sea. One ponders how they survived during storms in the small boats displayed that were used to fish the waters offshore.

Eventually it was time to continue down the road to Fortune. The boat for St. Pierre leaves from here. In less than two hours it conveniently delivers you to a different world. St. Pierre et Miquelon is all France managed to salvage of her vast North American Empire in the 1763 treaty ending the disastrous Seven Years War with Britain. Ironically in the long run the French turned out to be winners. Britain has long departed Canada, while France is still here. The little islands also give her a claim to the territorial seas around them, once rich with fish and potentially wealthy with oil and natural gas.

St. Pierre et Miquelon is technically part of France, and its residents are French citizens. They fly the French Tricolor, replaced the French franc with the euro (Canadian and sometimes American dollars are accepted), and mostly tune in French radio and television rather than that from Quebec. France provides their medical and judicial personnel, and the shops are filled with French goods, available at bargain prices, since they are not taxed locally. The islands do issue their own postage stamps, readily available, and popular with collectors.

Green Island, with its government-operated weather station, is the last piece of Canadian territory one encounters before sailing on toward the harbor of St. Pierre. The French colony is actually two islands, the larger dumbbell-shaped Miquelon that can boast of wild horses, many birds, and a lighthouse, but few people; with the much smaller St. Pierre where most of the inhabitants can be found in the town and administrative center bearing the same name as their island. As you enter St. Pierre harbor the hauntingly picturesque Ile aux Marins holds your attention. The little island and its tiny fishing village look as if they were just dropped out of the sky from France. At least this is the way tourists always hope the rural parts of the mother country might appear. However, no one comes outside to wave a friendly greeting. The village was abandoned in the early 1960s. It is carefully preserved, but only as a sort of museum.

As we went through the simple immigration procedures, I asked the French government official to please stamp my passport, which was not an automatic procedure. He cheerfully obliged and remarked there was a fifty-franc fee, a bit of local bureaucratic humor. From the dock it was only a short walk through town to the Hotel Robert, where most of my fellow passengers and I were staying. While you can get there in about two minutes, caution is in order as downtown St. Pierre traffic is surprisingly heavy. Where all these folks were going in their Renaults and Citroens I had no idea. The entire island of St. Pierre is probably no more than eight kilometers long.

The Hotel Robert is small, but at that time it was the island's largest and among its finest places to stay. During the Prohibition era it was a favorite haunt of Al Capone, and I wondered if my comfortable room might have on occasion been his. The friendly proprietors were happy to tell you about the hotel and maintained in one room a fascinating little museum filled with relics of shipwrecks and the Prohibition days. It is definitely worth a visit.

Prohibition played a significant part in the history of St. Pierre. Large ships from Canada and Britain would deliver whiskey and other spirits to the island. One building, still standing near the little airport, was among those that served as a warehouse for these goods, which arrived quite legally. On the island the merchandise was reloaded onto smaller, faster boats that could swiftly and more safely make illegal deposits along the East Coast of the United States to quench the thirst of speakeasy patrons and others deprived of desired drink. Business thrived. One of St. Pierre's sights is the so-called Cutty Sark Cottage, entirely constructed from wood used in crates for transporting whiskey bottles.

Another delight of St. Pierre is its food, cuisine as fine as you will find in France. With fondness I still recall a Coquille St. Jacques from a pleasant little restaurant near the waterfront. Wandering the streets of town is another enjoyable way to spend some time here, and except in the very heart of town the traffic disappears. You do in fact feel as if you are exploring a delightful French community. Possibly a visit to the *boulangerie* for pastry might appeal. You can also stop at a sidewalk cafe or dodge the vehicles and visit the Place General de Gaulle, near the post office. Here French President Charles de Gaulle delivered a brief speech after making a very controversial one in Montreal encouraging the sovereignty movement, as he proclaimed *"Vive le Quebec libre!"* There is also a museum and a small cathedral worth exploring.

A tour of the island can be conveniently arranged and only takes around an hour. From Pointe du Diament there are lovely views of the town and the largely uninhabited island interior. Nearby is the island cemetery with its partially above ground concrete vaults, strangely equipped with a porthole. No one seems to know why they were built this way, but perhaps it offers some sort of comfort to the living to peer in and see the caskets of one's ancestors resting undisturbed.

You can fly to St. Pierre from St. John's or Nova Scotia. It is best to be very flexible if you decide to arrive this way. Flights are not scheduled every day and sometimes must be cancelled entirely because of fog. I left the way I arrived, by boat. The trip back to Fortune was uneventful except for a much-appreciated whale sighting. On the way back to St. John's I readjusted to my normal environment. I stopped in Marystown at the McDonalds and put all thoughts of Coquille St. Jacques out of my mind.

For more information about this bit of France in North America you can visit the following web site: (http://www.st-pierre-et-miquelon.com/ english/index.php).

The Plains of Abraham (Parc des Champs-de-Bataille): The Quest for Dignity

There is no Biblical connection with the Plains of Abraham. The area was actually named for Abraham Martin, a pilot on the St. Lawrence River, which flows below past Cap Diamant, Quebec City's highest point. Here you will also find the Citadelle, a massive fortress begun by the French, completed by the British, and the oldest one in North America still in use. It is home to the Royal 22nd Regiment, an entirely French-speaking unit. The Plains were the site of the decisive battle for control of North America in 1759. British General Wolf engaged the French General Montcalm. Both died here, both have monuments commemorating their sacrifices, but the British were the only winners. France surrendered nearly all its North American territories. No doubt the inhabitants of what had been New France believed their subjection to British rule would be brief, and soon they would be exchanged for land elsewhere that the British would find more desirable and that France no longer wanted. As we have seen, that was not to be.

So today the Plains of Abraham occupy one of the most prominent spots in the most French city in the entire Western Hemisphere. They have, without anyone really intending it to happen, become something of a reminder to a people that they were both defeated and abandoned. As I walked across the battlefield, now a peaceful park, thoughts of ancient Greeks fighting Persians kept coming to my mind. The Persians never could understand the Greek love and willingness to sacrifice for freedom. Should not being ruled well be good enough?

Perhaps some of English Canada does not yet understand the soul of the *habitant*. Quebec, because it was ruled well by Britain, remained loyal to the Crown during the American Revolution, despite efforts by the Revolutionaries to bring it into the conflict. Stories persist that some elderly French families used to keep portraits of Queen Victoria in their home, as English ones tended to do. Down through the years there have been times of strain between the two nationalities, such as over the execution of Louis Riel and the disagreement over conscription in both World Wars, but the loyalty of French Canada to the country cannot seriously be questioned. So what is the problem?

I sense it lies deeper. Being ruled well is fine, but it is never really enough. Unless you possess your dignity, are assured that you are the equal of everyone else, you are not truly free. Possibly the story of Quebec separatism is as much the story of a quest for dignity as it is an effort to protect language or culture. When there is the certainty that one's dignity is respected within the soul of the nation, not just within its laws, the struggle will come to an end. The unanswered question is does that respect come within the Canadian soul or that of an independent Quebec. Eventually we will receive the answer.

Where Worlds Collide?

The Canadian Museum of Civilization is a grand place to visit. No place relates the Canadian story any better. You can lose yourself in totem polls from the Pacific Northwest, beautiful and moving Inuit sculpture and prints, and various exhibits that unfold the country's history from the earliest beginnings to the present. Even the building itself has a magnetic attraction about it. Architect Douglas Cardinal intended its flowing lines to serve as a reminder of the immensity and diversity of the country.

Musee Canadien des Civilisations sits on the north bank of the Ottawa River in Hull, Quebec. Across the street and on those beyond are scenes typical of French Canada and in some cases even of France itself. On the south bank of the river directly opposite the museum are the very impressive, very English Gothic buildings of Parliament in Ottawa. At least symbolically the museum sits astride the boundary of the two Canadas, one French the other English. Yet here there seems to be mostly harmony. You move from one world to the other peacefully, walking across a bridge or taking a taxi. Hull and the surrounding communities are a sort of high-tech Canadian Silicon Valley. Real estate values are rising, and there is a good deal of prosperity, as well as support for the present federal system of government. My taxi driver remarked that his family always speaks French at home, but they do not want separatism. Too much of the local economy is the result of the federal capital's presence in Ottawa to want that to happen. Others must feel the same way, since the Ottawa Valley tended to vote against sovereignty in the 1995 Quebec referendum on the question. Until their employer complained, even some employees of the separatist Bloc Quebecois political party felt quite comfortable living in Ontario, where costs were cheaper than on the Quebec side of the river.

So, perhaps worlds do not have to collide after all. Maybe the museum actually does present the history of many people who in some way even they cannot precisely define are one people. Maybe it is a symbol that the dream is and can be a reality.

Churchill, Manitoba: Looking for Miss Congeniality

It was my last day in Churchill, and except for the small, stuffed one in the outstanding Inuit museum I had not seen a polar bear. There were quite a few things I had done, such as visit Fort Prince of Wales, constructed by the Hudson's Bay Company in the 18th century to defend the fur trade, and which the French ultimately did capture. I had experienced the enchantment of hearing the beluga whales sing through underwater microphones as they swam around our boat in the tidal waters of the Churchill River. To the astonishment of some of the local residents who spotted my moment of temporary insanity, I had even gone wading in the waters of Hudson Bay, something I had long threatened to do if I was ever fortunate enough to get the opportunity. I had seen the Aurora Borealis, or Northern Lights, which perform as spectacularly here as anywhere in the world. I had managed to arrive in town on a white-knuckle flight from Thompson, Manitoba, in the midst of a howling storm that gave me a respect for bush pilots I will never forget. Now here I was in what proudly proclaims itself the "Polar Bear Capital of the World." I heard plenty of bear stories. I constantly came across visitors and residents who did announce bear sightings. But I had seen no bear.

To be fair to the bears, it was a little early. One comes to Churchill in the winter for the best of the Aurora, July and early August for the whales, and October through mid-November for bears. Once Hudson Bay is frozen enough the bears will depart land for the ice to devote most of their time to seal hunting. While it was early, it was not impossible. An occasional bear might be spotted by late July moving toward the shore in anticipation of better days (from its perspective, not that of the seal). Now it was August, and more bears than usual for this time of year were being reported. I remained hopeful.

I boarded the tundra buggy, a unique made-in-Churchill vehicle that looks something like a cross between a school bus and a monster truck, and asked our driver if he could guarantee a bear. He wisely remarked that when it came to bears there never were any guarantees. We headed out across the tundra, east of town. Our host would occasionally point out an unusual bird, a delicate lichen or similar flora and fauna, which also make Churchill a favorite destination for tourists in search of the rare and unusual. As we went over land and through small ponds he expertly drove the buggy across old trails, in order to prevent damage to the delicate terrain, where nature may need a century to erase a footprint.

Finally we reached a spot close to the shore of the Bay. We waited. We waited some more. Eventually she came, lumbering across the terrain in a slow, dainty fashion. Here was very clearly a polar bear. Those with expert knowledge on such matters said based on her size she was about two years old. I noticed she did not seem frightened by the intrusion of our weird craft and even approached it in a friendly manner. Evidently some who had been on earlier tours had already spotted her. In fact she had earned the name of "Miss Congeniality," because of her willingness to make an appearance when no other bear would bother.

She put on a nice show until we had to leave. I rode back to town on buggy and connecting bus with a warm glow inside. I had accomplished one of the things I had come here to do. Upon our arrival I tipped the driver and thanked him for making it all happen. Rumors were circulating that perhaps some caribou meat was tied to the bottom of the buggy. If so, I did not care and did not want to know. "Miss Congeniality" would always be mine.

I was happy I did not have to fly. That night I boarded the train that would take me back to Winnipeg. As Via Rail's *Hudson Bay* journeyed across the silent tundra, the stars shone with heavenly brilliance in the ink-black sky. The Aurora Borealis began its spectacular show complete with ribbons and curtains in the midst of the Pleiades meteor shower. All of this was reflected in the countless small ponds that dotted the tundra as we continued southward. Perhaps out there in the darkness, in her own way, "Miss Congeniality" was enjoying nature's all-star show as much as I.

Canora in the Morning

They are rapidly disappearing, but until recently almost every Manitoba and Saskatchewan prairie town had its distinctive grain elevator somewhere near the railroad tracks. The Canadian style is different from those you find in the American Midwest, and if you had somehow come across one when you had no idea where you were, the mystery of your location would be cleared up instantly. Now they are going, being replaced by fewer but much larger and more efficient, if less romantic, facilities. As my train from Churchill made its way south, tundra gave way to forest, and after a night and almost full day of travel forest began to give way to the plains and the towns that dot them. The grain elevators began to appear as we rumbled across the provincial boundary between Manitoba and Saskatchewan shortly before nightfall.

Periodically we stopped and discharged a few of our passengers. I have mentioned these folks before, but please permit me to reflect on that just a bit more. Some of these people I had gotten to know, a few even well. They were mostly Saskatchewan wheat farmers touring Churchill at the invitation of the Hudson Bay Route Association, in its efforts to promote shipping wheat to Europe through the Port of Churchill.

The farmers and their families were a most impressive lot. Agriculture on the prairies has gone "high tech" with well-educated growers using computers and the Internet to monitor grain futures prices. Above all these are people with an unusual degree of courage and perhaps just a bit of the gambler's mentality. As I previously noted, they marveled at the size of the current crop while at the same time worrying about the danger of an early frost before harvest. Some years farming the prairies brings a bonanza. Others it reaps only pain, heartache, and debt. Families looking for more safety and certainty have left. Some quit because they did not have the capital that modern farm machinery requires and realized that modern farming demands the machines if it is to be profitable. Farms have become fewer and larger in the effort to make them more efficient.

Through all this they manage to remain largely an optimistic and friendly lot, willing to break bread together, willing to answer countless questions, and willing to try to reveal the answer as to why some people love this way of life in spite of the sweat, the potential discouragement, and the crap shoot to some extent it will always be.

We went further southward. Folks continued to disembark at lonely stations as night deepened. Most of this group was from the area around Canora, a town I must admit I never knew existed before this journey. We finally reached there about three in the morning. I watched them leave, descending to the lighted station platform beside the train. Some greeted waiting friends or family. Others carried baggage to parked cars or trucks. They disappeared rather quickly into the night as the train pulled slowly away. I knew I would never see them again, but before their departure they had given me a glimpse, even if briefly, into the true soul of the Canadian prairies. I would carry that with me as I departed the railroad station in Winnipeg the next morning.

True North at Thirty Thousand Feet

The airline industry deserves some sympathy. Unstable fuel prices, crowded airports, and the World Trade Center tragedy have not made their lot an easy one. Nevertheless, I must utter a complaint. In-flight films are tools of the industry for anesthetizing passengers during those long hours when there is little else to do. No doubt many enjoy the show. They care not that if you have a window seat, and the weather is cooperating, you have a better one just outside. But why deprive those who opt for this alternative form of entertainment by requiring us to lower the window shades? This order may even come on night flights when the claim that outside light interferes with viewing is totally unrealistic. But sometimes they do not bother, sometimes enforcement is rather lax, and almost always you can quickly sneak an occasional peak. The show does go on.

Some day I intend to tour Canada's northern latitudes on foot. For now I will have to settle for that view from the cabin, while totally ignoring the newsreel, the pitch for in-flight shopping, and even the main feature. I am determined to see Canada, parts that are not quite as convenient as those farther south.

The immensity of the land is overwhelming. Mile after mile slips by; vast acreage of forest, punctuated with lakes, fills the view. Occasionally a road breaks the pattern, or possibly some sign of settlement, lessening for the moment the feeling of isolation and solitude. It may be northern Ontario, Manitoba, or Saskatchewan, beyond the areas where most folks live and work. With luck you may get a quick glimpse of some economic activity, probably mining, timber, or hydroelectric power. Mostly there is the stillness, the emptiness, the encounter with something actually too big and encompassing, something that can only be experienced, never fully understood, and certainly not controlled. Probably few would grasp its power. Better they watch the movie.

Continue northwest and province gives way to territory, the Northwest Territories, but the landscape seems much the same. Perhaps in places the trees seem somewhat thinner, although this is still well below tree line, where forest does give way to tundra. However, there is a psychological difference. The southern boundary of the Northwest Territories lies at 60 degrees north latitude. Many veterans of the Canadian Arctic believe "True North" begins "north of 60."

The continuity of the physical landscape is broken by the approach of Great Slave Lake, a seemingly endless body of water, teeming with fish, and actually smaller than Great Bear Lake, further north. I search in vain for a view of the territorial capital, Yellowknife, but it lies too far north to come into view. Eventually something almost as intriguing does make an appearance, the fabled Mackenzie Highway, which bears the name of two persons who made Canadian history. In 1789 Sir Alexander Mackenzie became the first European to traverse the land we call Canada and to explore the great river that bears his name. The other Alexander Mackenzie was elected prime minister in 1874. Yellowknife and the other Great Slave Lake communities lost some of their remoteness when the highway was begun in the late 1950s during the administration of Prime Minister John Diefenbaker. It is their lifeline to the South.

Some of the activity around Fort Providence, just west of the lake, comes into view. A short distance south of here the road forks. The branch already encountered goes up to Yellowknife. The other stretches westward on the way to Fort Simpson and beyond. Still further south and east there is another fork some distance after the highway leaves Alberta, with one branch going toward Fort Providence and the other to Hay River on the south shore of Great Slave Lake.

More or less following the course of the Mackenzie River, the highway approaches Fort Simpson in the western part of the Northwest Territories. I leave it near there, but it continues northwest on to Wrigley. At Wrigley it ends, well part of the year anyway. During the frigid winter the Mackenzie River freezes so solidly that plows are able to open up an ice road on the frozen surface, one strong enough to stand the weight of large trucks. They can travel all the way to the pioneer oil field at Norman Wells and on to remote Fort Good Hope. An eastern link makes it possible to reach Great Bear Lake. Ironically the harshness of the Canadian Arctic winter actually lessens the isolation of some communities. In parts of Labrador a similar situation exists where some settlements are most easily reached by snowmobile.

West of Fort Simpson the landscape begins to change. The Mackenzie Mountains come into view and dominate the scenery all the way to the border of the Yukon Territory where the companion Selwyn Mountains take over. Among the Selwyns are individual mountains still with glaciers, and both chains are a continuation of the Rockies. This is rugged and majestic land. One feels the plane is flying too low as these peaks reach up to challenge it. The Mackenzie range seems much higher than the unnamed summit that reaches 9098 feet or Mount Sir James McBrien at 9062 feet. Some of the more southern Selwyns are able to attain altitudes of almost 9700 feet. You sense the obstacles prospectors throughout the Northwest Territories and the Yukon have faced over the years as they sought the elusive fortunes of the area. The mountains give up their treasures only at a very high price, if at all, as many an adventurer who sought his dream found out, after it was too late. Still, there is wealth to be discovered, and the modern economies of the territories are the benefactors.

Continue further, reach the Coast Ranges of the southwest corner of the Yukon, and you find the tallest prize of all, Mount Logan, Canada's highest summit at 19,856 feet. But that will be saved for another time, as must the seemingly infinite miles of territory stretching north to the shores of the Arctic Ocean and eventually further, almost to the North Pole itself. Truth North remains elusive, a prize for only the few. Those who have answered her call learn to respect her and never to forget her.

The above was a composite of several flights that have taken me into remote parts of Canada I otherwise would not have had the opportunity to see. This same technique has also enabled me to "tour" some areas of Quebec, and the Atlantic provinces that might not have been immediately accessible by more conventional travel methods. Actually I have found it works well anywhere and has permitted me to "visit" places as different as Borneo and the Channel Islands even though they were not my intended destinations. I highly recommend it to you, particularly if you have already seen the film. Do not forget to request a window seat.

Banff Springs Hotel: Checking Out May Be Hard to Do

Many first-time visitors to Canada probably make their initial destination the Canadian Rockies. Why not? Banff and Jasper National Parks in Alberta, along with adjacent Kootenay and Yoho National Parks, across the border in British Columbia, have been a United Nations UNESCO World Heritage Site since 1985. The beauty of the area exceeds all the superlatives that might be attempted in an unsuccessful effort to capture the essence of this land. If heaven does not look something like this, it certainly should.

I was in Calgary on the weekend. The places I needed to go and the people I needed to see would not be available until Monday. That was fortunate. There was time and an excuse for a bus tour, as I was not in the mood to rent a car and drive, especially since there was the possibility of snow later in the day. There was only one available, to Banff. I took it.

The approach to Banff can be enjoyable enough. Occasionally there may be signs of Alberta's oil and gas industries, the industries that have made this one of the most prosperous areas in Canada. Traversing what was once the famed Cochrane Ranch, near the town of Cochrane is a reminder that at one time in these parts raising cattle was king. In 1881 Senator Matthew Cochrane of Montreal began to create a huge ranching empire in southwestern Alberta. His holdings were actually in two parcels and totaled some 334,500 acres. Today the land has been divided, and mixed farming has replaced much of the cattle, but an impressive monument of a cowboy on horseback serves as a reminder of this historic enterprise.

Eventually one reaches the park and the mountains. There is much here to delight even the traveler with just a few hours to spend in this majestic setting. The mysterious hoodoos, odd column-like rock formations carved by erosion are a delight, and the beginnings of the park's development can be explored at the hot sulphur springs which attracted early visitors convinced of their curative powers. If eating and shopping are on your itinerary, then the town of Banff offers a variety of opportunities.

Probably the most photographed spots in the park are serene Lake Louise and the Banff Springs Hotel. One of the most famous of the former Canadian Pacific Hotels, today it is operated by Fairmont Hotels and Resorts, one of the five companies to emerge from the breakup of Canadian Pacific Limited. Our accommodating driver takes us to the hotel and provides time for a brief visit. On the way he relates the bizarre story of the construction of the structure. For a time the architect had to be absent from the construction site. When he returned he discovered much to his shock and horror that someone had reversed the plans, and the hotel was being built backwards! With some difficulty he managed to reverse things to a considerable extent. The unforgettable views the hotel offers were preserved, but at the cost of halls, passageways, staircases, and entrances that do not seem to go where they should go. He warned it was easy to get lost inside.

I had to explore this place. It was just too impressive to not do so. As I entered I was not disappointed. The traditional grandeur of the establishment is just what one always hoped it would be, and perhaps you are transported back in time to a more elegant and leisurely era, at least for those who could afford resorts such as this in days past. I delight in my visit, but I must soon leave. Only, I discover I cannot. In just a few minutes I have become hopelessly lost, trying several different exit strategies, but all in vain. I spot a maid and ask for directions. I suspect this is not the first time she has answered the call for help. She casually points the way, and soon I am back on the bus, relieved to be finally free but also somewhat pleased I had such an adventure.

The ride back to Calgary is rather peaceful. As we approach the city we pass by the site of the Winter Olympic Games. By now the promised snow has also arrived, gently and quietly covering everything in a mantle of white. I had not expected snow this late in spring. Somehow it adds to the splendor of the day.

Victoria: An Unusual Study in "Family History"

I had always said if I got to Seattle I was going to go on to Victoria, the capital of British Columbia. Not that I have any objections to Seattle, which is a very fascinating city with fabled Pike Market, the Pioneer and International Districts, and fairly convenient access to Mount Rainier National Park. But I wanted to see Victoria, which some proclaim as the most "British" city in all of Canada. There are two ferry lines that make access to Vancouver Island (not to be confused with the mainland city of Vancouver) very easy, and in a few hours you can depart from downtown Seattle and arrive in Victoria harbor. Dominating this part of the city is another former Canadian Pacific property, the much beloved Empress Hotel. She offers formal elegance, comfortable rooms, gourmet dining, and the popular tradition of high tea. This may sometimes be a bit overrun with tourists, but it should be done at least once. It is a most civilized custom, truly a part of Victoria, and the hope of meeting an occasional celebrity is not unrealistic.

A very short distance away from the Empress, are the British Columbia Parliament Buildings and the Provincial Museum. Both are well worth a visit, and it is tempting to linger at the museum with its many intriguing exhibits that so well relate the history of the province. Our ultimate goal, however, is Thunderbird Park, next door to the museum. Here you will find a replica of a Haida Indian Big House. If you are there at the right times you will discover it serves as a studio for Indian carvers who continue the time-honored art of creating the totem poles for which the Pacific Northwest is famous. You can see older ones in the museum, but watching one before your eyes slowly "emerge from the wood" is to sense a different time and world from the one we usually experience. Contrary to what some people believe, totems are not religious symbols. If you can pardon a gentle pun, they are really more like the family tree, relating the traditions and history of the Indian bands. As such they are reminders of First Nations' history and culture, things that here they are willing to share with others provided they have a genuine interest.

The totems are symbols of the diversity and the age of the Canadian nation. Its story actually began even before the Vikings landed at L'Anse-aux-Meadows and has a richness that is not easy to forget. I feel very privileged that I have been able to journey across this immense land, one that never ceases to fill me with awe and wonder. There are many more tales that could have been included in this collection of memories, such as discovering the Acadian culture of Prince Edward Island, pondering

Fort York, where the city of Toronto began, or dining with Canadian customs officials while we are stranded between flights at Thompson in northern Manitoba. They cannot all be told, but one very special experience just has to be related. So before going on to other things, please join me near the top of the world.

**Icebergs on their way south to Newfoundland
floating off the coast of Labrador**

The old Hudson Bay Company outpost at Cartwright, Labrador

The beginning of the western section of the Trans-Labrador Highway at Happy Valley-Goose Bay

The porthole graves in France's St. Pierre et Miquelon

The lighthouse at Peggy's Cove, Nova Scotia

A preserved Victorian era schoolroom at the Orwell Corner
Historic Village, Prince Edward Island

The famous Giant Flowerpots at Hopewell Cape, New Brunswick

Campaign posters compete for voters in a Québec City municipal election

Named for a governor of New France, the Montmorency Falls northeast
of Québec City are 50 percent higher than Niagara Falls.

Toronto's City Hall is a distinctive landmark for this largest of all Canadian cities.

The grave of Louis Riel, St. Boniface, Manitoba

Miss Congeniality inspects a Tundra Buggy near Churchill, Manitoba

The splendors of Banff National Park, Alberta

**Keeping English traditions alive: Lawn Bowling in
Victoria, British Columbia**

Preserving the heritage of the First Nations:
Totems in Victoria, British Columbia

NUNAVUT VIA BEIJING

Even that word "Nunavut" conjures up almost mystical connotations. "Our Land," the Inuit have proudly and properly named it in their own language. Among my dreams was one of exploring Nunavut. It even led to applying for a research permit from the Territorial Government. Because they are carefully protective of potentially fragile aboriginal cultures, the Nunavut authorities require a license before any research may be conducted in the territory. My application was approved. The permit was granted. The hoped-for necessary funding was not forthcoming. The project died. It seemed destined to remain that way. Then when it was not anticipated, an opportunity for at least a glimpse of this special place magically appeared.

We were sitting in an airplane at O'Hare Field in Chicago, getting as ready as one can for the seemingly endless flight to Beijing. As usual, I had claimed a window seat. Shortly after takeoff the captain announced we would get to China earlier than originally scheduled since he had been fortunate enough to claim a polar route that would take us closer to the North Pole than I ever expected to be. Suddenly I knew that if the weather cooperated I could have my chance.

It seemed that the opportunity might disappear as rapidly as it had arrived. By the time we reached the Upper Peninsula of Michigan heavy clouds obscured all but an occasional glimpse of the terrain below. Lake Superior was totally covered, and Northern Ontario was encountering a similar fate. For just a moment or two a break would reveal the white snow-covered surface far below. Disappointment would be an understatement.

Finally we arrive at Hudson Bay, and with it somewhat better conditions. The ice that coats the bay all winter was showing signs of cracking, sometimes in zig-zags, sometimes in rectangular shapes, and in still others that defy description. In one spot a rectangular slice of open water had already appeared. I had seen the bay once before, and ice free, during an August journey to Churchill, Manitoba. I had walked on a beach and even been crazy enough to wade briefly in the frigid waters. However, it will be July before the ice breaks up in earnest and ships can once again use the port of Churchill during the brief summer season.

We continue further north. The weather also continues to improve while the surface below prepares to take on a more hostile appearance. We make landfall to the west of Southampton Island and continue northward toward the remote Boothia Peninsula and Somerset Island. The landscape takes on an indescribable surrealist, almost supernatural appearance. Mountains force their way through the thick snow. Here and there mysterious valleys and gorges appear along with dark-brown splotches that have surrendered their white blankets to what must be relentless winds. One cannot help wondering how anyone could survive in such a hostile-looking place.

We have made our way through the Keewatin Region, then along the east coast of the peninsula and island as we continue northward, alternating between ice and land. At one point close to a shoreline we reach a substantial patch of open water and pieces of rather thin ice. The Arctic Ocean does have some bizarre spots known as polynyas that are ice free even in the winter when the entire sea is normally frozen. Perhaps this may be one of those, or maybe it is a sign that summer is finally drawing closer, and some of the ocean will awaken briefly from its ice-bound rigidity, though large portions remain frozen the entire year.

Then the impossible comes into view. Far below on the southern coast of an island is what is clearly a settlement. In this latitude there is only one place it can be, the hamlet of Resolute Bay on the south shore of

Cornwallis Island. Why would anyone, even the hardy Inuit, select such a place to settle? That is a question that produces a very disturbing answer.

Cornwallis Island lies about 400 kilometers south of the North Magnetic Pole, and is one of the highly isolated and largely uninhabited group known as the Queen Elizabeth Islands. Resolute Bay, or Qausuittuq as the Inuit call it, is located on that fabled body of water known as the Northwest Passage. For centuries, mariners dreamed of a shortcut, an all water route to the Orient and the riches that Asian trade could bring to Europe. But Nature was to have the last word. The passage through the Parry Channel can be done during the summer with difficulty, provided you possess an icebreaker. Some of it remains frozen all year.

The Canadian government established a weather station at Resolute Bay in 1947. Today the town of 200 plus souls is surviving nicely, perhaps even thriving. It has become the focal point for those doing Arctic research and tourists headed for the Pole. Mining sites are also supplied out of here, and Resolute Bay can boast of being the world's most Northern city with regularly scheduled airline service, though at times you may have to wait several days for your flight while the weather clears.

The situation was not always this bright. In the fall of 1953 three Inuit families from Pond Inlet (Mittimatalik) on Baffin Island and fourteen families from Inukjuak, Quebec, were relocated by the Government of Canada to Resolute Bay and to the even further northern community of Grise Fiord (Ausittuq), on southern Ellesmere Island. Supposedly the hunting would be better in their new locations. In reality these "Internal Exiles," as they came to call themselves, were victims of the Cold War. Under International Law the only clearly accepted way of claiming sovereignty over territory is to effectively occupy it. In the empty North, Canada was fearful of possible Soviet incursions or even potential claims by the United States or Denmark, which has sovereignty over Greenland. The Inuit were to be used as pawns to prove "effective occupation." Such severe locations are even difficult for the Inuit, who against fierce odds managed to survive and now even see these places as home. What they want is a silent Ottawa to take responsibility for what was done to them and why, as well as compensation to insure the well being of their descendants. Their demands do not appear unreasonable.

We continue west from Resolute through the Queen Elizabeth Islands over the northern coast of Bathurst Island, then the southwestern edge of Elief Rignes Island, site of the North Magnetic Pole, soon leaving the territorial waters of Nunavut, and into the open Arctic Sea. At our closest point we will be no more than 300 to 400 miles from the actual North Pole. Here there is no summer thaw. However, deep crevices can be seen in the ice, and though it is difficult to judge from such a high altitude, the distance to the water below the cap may be as much as 100 to 150 feet, or even more. Across that barren ice field we go on, with nothing but the cracks varying the landscape. Eventually we reach the New Siberian Islands and then head south across the vast Siberian wilderness. The rugged peaks of the Verchojanskij Chrebet come into view. This is a land of snow, ice, and mountain, eventually giving way to forest and snow. We cross what is most likely the Vil'uj River, which flows into the larger Lena, probably near the town of Verchnevil'ujsk, where for the first time since Resolute signs of human inhabitation are evident. A substantial bridge spans the river. Further south the Trans-Siberian Railroad and the newer Baykal-Amur line that runs north of it are spotted. While the Trans-Siberian spanned Russia by the 1890s, the Baykal-Amur, or BAM, rail link was not completed until the 1980s and was the last great construction project of the former Soviet Union.

Forest gives way to steppe before we cross the border into Mongolia. Brown is the order of the day, with little to break up that landscape except two small villages along the way to the Chinese Autonomous Region of Inner Mongolia. Residents in Beijing will tell you they suffer several dust storms a year that blow in from the Gobi Desert. What you see from the air confirms that, as green fertile fields do not appear until you are relatively close to the capital city. The Great Wall is reached, and soon after Beijing itself. The journey is over. Nunavut is far away, yet in some ways it is closer than it ever has been before.

THE CONTRIBUTION OF WOMEN
TO CANADIAN SOCIETY

The role that women played in the development of the Canadian nation is one even less known south of the border than that of the country itself. Yet, it is one that needs to be told, because it is a story of courage, sacrifice, and determination. Their contribution is one in which all Canadians can take pride.

If Americans had their heroines such as Betsy Ross and Molly Pitcher who supported the struggle for independence from Britain as strongly as any man, Canada can answer with the brave Laura Secord who helped save her country from a southern invasion. Escorted by Iroquois braves, she traveled through the woods and past enemy lines during the War of 1812 to warn British troops that "the Americans are coming." American forces had occupied Fort George on the southern shore of Lake Ontario, north of Buffalo, and posed a serious threat to Canada.

As the frontier expanded Westward, Canadian women again played a critical role. French Voyageurs engaging in the fur trade advanced forward by canoe, opening up new areas for settlement as they went. They married women from the Indian bands, and from these marriages the unique Metis society was born. Voyageur and Metis would be joined by families seeking opportunity in the prairie lands along the Red River in Manitoba and eventually Saskatchewan. The Red River ox cart became the symbol of these pioneer families, and women were of course a vital part of these courageous settlers. Even in traditional roles women played a key role in the development of the interior. The oldest building in St. Boniface, Manitoba, now part of Winnipeg, is the convent.

Just as in the United States, Canadian women had to struggle for the vote as well as property and other legal rights. They also sought educational and employment opportunities, better health conditions, and advancement for their children. Like their American counterparts, some of them became involved in these causes by first participating in the prohibition movement where they learned and refined their organizational and lobbying strategies The fight for the franchise had to be waged on two fronts, both the federal and provincial, since Canada is a federal country.

Again there is a parallel to the United States, as it was the American West that led the way. Wyoming earned the title of the Equality State in 1890 when it entered the Union and also became the first state to grant women the vote. Jeanette Rankin from Montana in 1916 became the first woman elected to Congress. In Canada the Western Prairie provinces of Manitoba, Saskatchewan, and Alberta extended the vote to women in 1916. Ontario and British Columbia followed the next year.

Credit for the breakthrough in part belongs to Nellie McClung (1873-1951), an early suffragist. Born and raised in Manitoba, she played a leading role in the Liberal party's 1914 campaign against the Conservatives, who had refused the suffrage. Although she moved to Alberta before the Liberal victory in 1915, the party went on to bring about the reform for which she had worked so tirelessly. In Alberta she worked for the suffrage, factory safety, and other reforms. Later she served in the provincial legislature and was a delegate to the League of Nations.

Quebec is a most interesting case. Women there had to wait until 1940 to receive the vote. The province's traditional culture did not undergo dramatic change until the Quiet Revolution of the 1960s turned both men and women in a more political, urban and secular direction away from the rural society of the past in which the church had played the leading institutional role. Until that time the rights of women, especially married women, were limited. Today Quebec is often one of the more liberal provinces in regard to gender issues.

As Nellie McClung had shown, the battle for the vote was not enough. Canadian women were determined to hold political office. By 1917 Alberta had two women in its provincial legislature. A bigger breakthrough came in 1921 when Agnes McPhail (1890-1954), running in a Saskatchewan riding, was elected to the federal Parliament. She fought to stop the decline in the rural way of life. In 1941 she became one of the first two women elected to the Ontario legislature, where she would remain until 1951. During this time she worked for women's civil rights and equal pay, and for the vote for the women of Quebec.

Women activists also took their fight to the courts. Probably the most critical effort was the Persons Case, which is officially known as Henrietta Muir Edwards v. Attorney General of Canada. In the 1920s a group of Western women, including Nellie McClung, and popularly known as the Famous Five, took the issue of appointment to the federal Senate to the Supreme Court of Canada. That body ruled that under the country's constitution, the British North America Act of 1867, women were not "qualified persons."

Until passage of the Supreme Court Act of 1949, appeals to the British Privy Council were permitted. The women took their case to the Judicial Committee of the Privy Council, and in 1929 it overturned the Court's decision. Prime Minister Mackenzie King immediately appointed Cairine Wilson as the nation's first woman Senator. Unfortunately for a number of years there were few similar appointments. However, the Persons Case continued to be a source of hope and inspiration. Today Canadian women's groups still sponsor "Persons' Day Breakfasts."

In recent decades women have made further progress in obtaining prominent posts in the federal government. In 1957 Ellen Fairclough became the first woman to serve in the federal cabinet, while the 1963 appointment of Judy LaMarsh made her the second. Bertha Wilson in 1982 was the first woman appointed to the Supreme Court, and in 1989 Beverly McLachlin was selected to serve as Chief Justice.

While it is largely a ceremonial post, the office of Governor General is one of distinction, since the person holding it is the Queen's personal representative when she is not in Canada. In 1984 Jean Sauve was the first woman to receive the honor of that appointment, while Chinese-Canadian Adrienne Clarkson was appointed in 1999.

Canada's present Governor General, Michaelle Jean, is in many ways not only a reminder of the contribution of women to Canadian society but also of the nature of the country itself. She was born in Port-au-Prince, Haiti, and with her family in 1968 fled the notorious Francois Duvalier's cruel dictatorship, finding refuge in Canada. Highly educated in both Canada and Europe, she speaks five languages and can read a sixth one. On September 27, 2005, she was inaugurated Governor General, the third woman to hold that post, the second immigrant, and the first of Afro-Caribbean descent. Sometimes misunderstood by both federalists and sovereignists, Michaelle Jean has sought to break down barriers and misunderstandings among Canada's various "solitudes," to try to help people of different regions and different backgrounds understand each other and the place of all of them in Canadian society. She is truly a Canadian in the finest sense of the word.

Although the United States has never had a woman President, Canada has had a woman Prime Minister. The Progressive Conservative party's Kim Campbell achieved the post in 1993 after Brian Mulroney's resignation. She was highly popular and respected both at home and abroad but later in the year lost an election, which was largely fought over the issue of the Goods and Services Tax (GST). She continues to ably serve Canada as one of its diplomats.

The New Democratic party has taken the lead in offering leadership of a major political party to women. Audrey McLaughlin was elevated to the post of party head in 1989. In 1995 Alexa McDonough followed her. Actually in the mid-1970s Flora MacDonald of the Progressive Conservative party appeared to be well on the way to becoming leader of that party until a number of delegates wearing Flora buttons failed to follow through by actually voting for her. She overcame this setback to go on and serve in the cabinets of Prime Ministers Joe Clark and Brian Mulroney.

At the provincial and local levels women have also made political accomplishments. Catherine Callbeck of Prince Edward Island in 1993 became the first woman premier. British Columbia and the Yukon and Northwest Territories have also had women in charge of their governments. Shirley McAlary as mayor of Saint John, New Brunswick, was head of the country's oldest incorporated city and the largest in the province. In Nunavut, where societal and technological changes have brought challenges to the traditional hunting and fishing roles of men, women have frequently been called upon to provide both stability and leadership in families, Inuit society, and government. Inuit women hold vital positions as teachers, administrators throughout the territory, and as artists in the thriving Inuit art market. One was appointed the country's ambassador to the Arctic Council. There is every reason to believe that women will continue to make significant contributions throughout the entire country in the years ahead.

There are of course problems. Women in both Indian and Metis society sometimes find themselves in a cultural and legal ambiguity that can make it difficult to resolve their personal identity. They may be called to live in two worlds, while not being fully a part of either one. In the mining communities of Labrador married women have been welcomed. The companies tended to see them as a stabilizing influence on the miners. Unmarried women were seen as just the opposite and discouraged from coming. As a general rule, the private sector has moved more slowly than government. Women still earn less than men, but the gap is narrowing, and the governments do have pay equity legislation. Better access to day care would also help.

The Charter of Rights and Freedoms, which is a critical part of the 1982 Federal Constitution, is valuable to Canadian women seeking to make their contribution to society. It guarantees rights under the Charter equally to both sexes. Provinces may not evade this by invoking the document's "notwithstanding clause" that does permit them to make exceptions to certain Charter provisions. In addition the rights of aboriginal peoples are also guaranteed equally to males and females. Other efforts at the federal level, such as the 1986 Employment Equity Act for Crown (government) corporations, have also been beneficial. At least in recent decades the courts have been supportive of women's rights as well. As a result of the Supreme Court's decision in the 1988

Morganteler Case there are no federal restrictions on abortion. At the federal level Canadian women would appear to have better legal guarantees of equality than their American counterparts. In some instances this is also true when comparing the provinces with the states.

The future for Canadian women should be one of opportunity and one where they continue to strengthen the country politically, economically, and culturally. If Canadian society has often been conservative, it has also shown it can be both tolerant and flexible. It welcomes contributions from all who have something to contribute. The Canadian past has ably demonstrated that women have helped to create the Canadian nation. Their efforts will be essential to the success of its future.

THE FIRST NATIONS

The term aboriginal peoples may be confusing to non-Canadians. It is not derogatory, and it is found in the Canadian Constitution. In Canadian usage the term means those who were among the founders of this nation but were not of European origin. They include Indians, Inuit, and Metis. The Metis, as we have seen, do trace their origins to the French Voyageurs who opened up the interior as well as the Indian bands of Canada. The Indians and Inuit were already here when the first Europeans arrived. All three of these groups have made their own unique contributions to the Canada we know today. Without them the country would be far less rich than it is now.

Unfortunately these peoples have often been misunderstood by outsiders and even by each other. The term First Nations is sometimes loosely applied to all of them, but is often reserved strictly for the Indian bands. They vastly prefer it to the term Indian and usually refer to themselves as bands rather than tribes. The Inuit, incorrectly known as Eskimos, are a very distinctly different people, with a language and culture of their own. Usage of the term Eskimo is evidence of the misunderstanding between the First Nations and the Inuit, whose name means "The People" in their Inuktitut language. As we have previously noted, Eskimo is an uncomplimentary Cree word meaning "eaters of raw flesh."

Generally where one finds Inuit living there will be few First Nations people, and the same situation is true in First Nations settlements. There have been some exceptions. Approximately 45,000 Canadians can trace their ancestry from more than one aboriginal group, but generally such cultures have not blended. In all probability this may be due to the fact that the North is not an easy land in which to survive. First Nations and Inuit at times competed for the same hunting and fishing areas, with nothing less than their survival at stake. It is not surprising that such a struggle produced tension between the two.

Today, with the establishment of the Territory of Nunavut, "Our Land," the Inuit enjoy a cultural security and to some extent even an economic one not found among the First Nations peoples or the Metis. Not all Inuit live in Nunavut. There are important Inuit communities in the Ungava area of northern Quebec as well as the Northwest Territories and Labrador. Not all residents of Nunavut are Inuit either. The territory is open to anyone wishing to live there. However, the *Nunavut Act* and the *Nunavut Land Claim Agreement Act* enacted by Parliament create a political and economic climate in which Inuit opportunities and culture may do well. We have previously mentioned there are major obstacles to overcome, but much has already been accomplished. Throughout Canada the approximately 52,000 Inuit are well represented by the Inuit Tapirisat of Canada.

For the Metis the situation is much more ambiguous. As a whole they are far more likely to be found in urban areas than either of the other two groups. As a result it may be easier for those who desire to assimilate to do so, but it is also much more difficult to maintain Metis identity, customs, and their distinct French dialect. Their national organization, the Metis National Council of Canada has the challenging task of seeking to represent its roughly 265,000 constituents.

Where the Metis can be found in some number their cultural presence is significant and may even be enjoying a revival. Probably this is most true in the St. Boniface section of Winnipeg, which is associated with the man of controversy Louis Riel, himself a Metis. Riel can be said to have fought and died for both Metis and First Nations in the Red River Rebellion of 1869-1870 and the North West or Saskatchewan Rebellion of 1884-1885. The situation for these peoples had become desperate with wanton destruction of the buffalo herds and the loss of their land. It was

Riel who sought to reverse the tide. Declared guilty of treason, and certainly not free of mistakes, he none-the-less remained a hero to those forgotten and disposed, who saw him as their only hope in a desperate struggle for justice. He remains so to this day.

It is perhaps the First Nations who face the most uncertainty in the future. They do indeed find themselves with favorable possibilities, but there are difficult challenges as well. In some ways this is not surprising. They have always faced a somewhat ambiguous situation.

There are over 540 bands in Canada occupying over 2,200 reserves. Some of these such as the Dene, Cree, Innu, Ojibway, and Mohawk, as well as others, are reasonably large in number. Many are relatively small, which adds to their potential vulnerability. The most important piece of federal legislation affecting all the bands is the Indian Act of 1876. It also has revealed the inevitable conflict resulting from a government whose primary objective was the assimilation of First Nations peoples into Canadian society and the struggle by these same persons to maintain their identity and culture. The results have sometimes been grim. Although it has now been amended numerous times, and often for the better, the Indian Act originally forbade many Indian dances and cultural customs, denied the vote to those who refused to assimilate, and made of the chiefs little more than agents of the federal government. Indian children were frequently taken against the will of their parents and placed in boarding schools. Unlike American Indians on reservations, the bands do not own the land set aside for their use. Not until 1960 could all First Nations peoples vote, and until 1985 a woman who married a white man or an Indian who gave up the rights the Indian Act did guarantee automatically lost her status as an Indian.

Under the Indian Act, persons fall into one of two categories. These are status and non-status. Non-status Indians are normally those not living on the reserves established by treaty with the bands. They have given up whatever rights and protection the Indian Act might offer. They are essentially treated like any other citizen of the country, though on the whole they do not enjoy as high a standard of living. The Native Council of Canada does seek to work for their rights. Status Indians under the Indian Act are registered as Indians with the federal government and usually live on reserves. Today of the approximately 960,000 Canadians who are of North American Indian origin, only a little under 290,000 live on reserves. The Indian Act does exempt them from federal, provincial, and territorial taxes on their reserve lands and grants certain other privileges. The most powerful of any aboriginal organizations, the Assembly of First Nations, ably represents the interests of status Indians. It has sought a recognition for them not unlike that desired by many in Quebec.

Status Indians have made progress. A dramatic shift in attitude toward all aboriginal peoples probably began around 1940 when many served in the nation's military. If they embraced the sacrifices the rest of the population was making then surely they were entitled to the same rights as everyone else. In 1969 federal Indian agents were withdrawn from the reserves, ending a kind of paternalism that had long outlived whatever purposes it may have originally had. By 1973 the First Nations had reclaimed the right to educate their children, and in 1988 were granted the right to levy their own property taxes on reserve lands. In 1996 thirteen First Nations and the federal government entered into the Framework Agreement on First Nations Land Management. This allows them to pass laws to develop, conserve, protect, and manage their land.

First Nations land claims are also being successfully negotiated with the provinces and territories, though much remains to be done before such matters are finally settled. However, British Columbia, which historically had been slow to deal with First Nations claims, has in recent years successfully negotiated some landmark settlements.

In 2002 the government of Quebec and the Grand Council of the Crees signed an agreement that not only gave to the Cree Nation compensation for their resources but a role in the future management of them. This "Peace of the Brave," among other things has enabled the creation of the Cree Development Corporation. Appointed mostly by Crees, this body plays a critical role in the economic and social development of the James Bay region, an area that is rich in hydroelectric resources. That the two parties were able to come together was particularly impressive in view of past Cree concerns about Quebec sovereignty being declared without their consent Quebec also has a 2002 agreement with the Inuit entitled Sanarrutik, the Inuktitut word meaning "Development Tool." It calls for cooperation on developing the hydroelectric potential of the Inuit area of Nunavik.

The courts in a numbers of instances have upheld traditional rights and claims, sometimes invoking the Constitutional Charter of Rights and Freedoms. Ironically the Charter has not only benefited the First Nations, it has also become a new source of potential conflict between them and the rest of Canada. As debate for further amendment or more likely drastic overhauling of the Indian Act increases, First Nations leaders fear that if the Charter is applied to them precisely the way it is to other Canadians, it could weaken or destroy traditional governmental and societal customs and practices. Change seems inevitable, but it may not come easily. However, there is no turning back. All aboriginal peoples have an indispensable role to play in Canada's future. The country cannot afford to leave them behind.

CANADA, THE UNITED STATES, AND THE WORLD

There was a time when many Canadians would have seen their country's foreign policy as mostly an echo emanating from London, although this was not true in all cases. For instance, Ottawa thought it should have received stronger British backing in its dispute with the United States over the Alaska boundary. Although Prime Minister Robert Borden joined the British delegation at the Paris Peace Conference in 1919, Canada signed the Versailles Treaty for itself and took its own seat in the League of Nations, the forerunner of the United Nations. The British Parliament's Statute of Westminster in 1931 also made it clear that dominions had complete control over their own foreign policy. Gradually, perhaps without being fully conscious of the process, Canada has developed a foreign policy which, while usually supportive of Britain and the United States, is truly its own and puts Canadian interests first, as would that of any fully sovereign country.

Sometimes these interests are defended in subtle but firm ways. March 2002 saw the Canadian government close the country's ports to ships of the Faeroe Islands, a small North Atlantic island group which is a self-governing region of Denmark. The reason was over fishing of shrimp and the resulting threat to Canadian fisheries. With 50,000 inhabitants the Faeroes are hardly a major threat to the Canadian economy, but the act was intended to serve as a warning to other, larger states that Canada has accused of similar activity. Later Estonia and several other nations received similar treatment.

Canada claims extensive amounts of Arctic waters as part of its sovereign territory. The seas in question often lie between the remote northern islands of Nunavut. While some other nations, including the United States, reject Canada's position and view the waters as international territory, the matter has not been a critical one since most are frozen much or all of the year. Other than an occasional and essentially friendly "showing of the flag" by the American Navy there has really been no challenge to the Canadian view. With global warming now a planetary trend, there has been increasing concern in Ottawa that these passages are annually thawing sooner and in some cases could even be attractive to international shipping. In the summer of 2002 the Canadian Navy made its first sailings into Arctic waters in thirteen years. The express purpose was to reinforce national sovereignty and train its sailors. Although lacking adequate equipment, the Navy anticipates future northern exercises and can be expected to lobby for the necessary ships to do the job properly.

The decade of the 1990s and the start of the new millennium were accompanied by a Canadian foreign policy intent on playing a growing role in international cooperation. Perhaps the country's proudest achievement was the 1997 treaty that banned the use of land mines. Canada was the initiator of this treaty and played an indispensable role in bringing about its passage. Over 125 nations have already ratified it, while still others have signed it and are considering ratification. The treaty is now in force among those countries that have ratified or acceded to it.

By 2002 enough governments had ratified the 1998 Rome Statute, which called for the establishment of an International Criminal Court under the auspices of the United Nations. The Court's purpose is to try cases dealing with war crimes, crimes against humanity, and genocide. Canada was the fourteenth country to ratify the treaty, but the first to both ratify and pass implementing legislation. As such Canada is being hailed as a leader in the effort to establish the international body.

On another international agreement the Canadian position is less united. This is the Kyoto accord, intended to cut greenhouse gas emissions and slow global warming. Canada promptly signed the agreement, with the federal government then moving in a serious manner to support ratification. Prime Minister Chretien promised a vote in Parliament before the end of 2002, and in December the House of Commons gave him the favorable decision he desired. His Liberal party received support from the New Democrats and Bloc Quebecois for the treaty. The Alliance and Progressive Conservatives opposed it. Several provinces, including Manitoba and Quebec along with the Yukon Territory have also been supportive. The remaining provincial and territorial governments have had some reservations, fearing negative economic impacts. Alberta and Newfoundland and Labrador opposed ratification of the treaty in its present form, and Nova Scotia has also been unhappy. All three provinces fear it could hurt their economies in which petroleum and natural gas production are major contributors. They also feel they are at an additional competitive disadvantage if the United States continues to oppose the treaty. Despite the concerns, the Canadian Parliament ratified the treaty on December 17, 2005. Canada was also the host for a 2005 meeting of the ratifying nations. The present Conservative government does have reservations about Kyoto, and no doubt debate on it will continue to be lively, but many Canadians seem committed to making it work.

There are other signs of an activist foreign policy in recent years. Canadian and Russian companies have signed business agreements. Both governments are making efforts to promote bilateral trade. France and Canada are working together toward the development of the oil and gas fields between Canadian territory and the islands of St. Pierre et Miquelon. A summer 2002 poll also found Canadians in favor of efforts by the developed countries to aid the poorer ones.

In the future Canada should be expected to pursue similar policies to those we have noted. The country is quite capable of looking after its political and economic interests and will continue to play a positive role in international cooperation and conciliation. Such a tradition is actually quite well established. Former Prime Minister Lester Pearson is credited with the invention of United Nations peacekeeping in the 1950s.

If nothing else, Canadian support for the Land Mines treaty, International Criminal Court, and Kyoto accord, should point out the country's policies are truly its own and not made in U.S.A. Washington, for its own reasons, opposes all three of these treaties. Regardless, there are many areas where American and Canadian understanding and cooperation have been very positive. Given their long, peaceful border, extensive trade relations, and the cultural affinity of the two states, they both have a lot to gain by working together as much as possible.

One of the greatest demonstrations of Canadian friendship the United States ever received occurred when more than eighty thousand Canadians, including Prime Minister Jean Chretien and Governor General Adrienne Clarkson, along with American Ambassador Paul Celucci, gathered on Parliament Hill to mourn the victims of the World Trade Center attack. Several months later, in December, thousands of Canadians came to New York to show their solidarity with the city. Given the currency exchange rate at the time, they did this in spite of the financial sacrifice involved.

Canadian efforts went beyond symbolic demonstrations. During the war in Afghanistan, the country's diplomats made quiet contacts with countries such as Iran and Syria, whose relations with the United States are poor, to secure their cooperation or at least tolerance for the effort to oust the Taliban from power. Canada contributed naval and ground forces to the Afghan operation and worked with the United States to improve border security while at the same time keeping any disruption to commerce and other legitimate activity to a minimum. More needs to be done in this regard. Both are committed to doing it. Along with many other countries, Canada has sought to shut off the financial resources of terrorist organizations.

The relationship has not been perfect. Washington complains Canada does not spend enough on defense. Ottawa criticizes American tendencies toward unilateralism and along with others questioned the wisdom of invading Iraq. Still, the two governments hold joint military exercises, remain good NATO partners, and cooperate in a variety of international efforts. There is no reason to believe this will change in the future.

If there is one single thing that continually makes Canada unhappy in its relations with the United States it is the 1996 Cuban Liberty and Democratic Solidarity Act, commonly known as the Helms-Burton law. The law took various pieces of legislation and administrative orders that restricted or totally prohibited trade with Cuba and in effect combined them and made them applicable to the Trading with the Enemy Act of 1917. The Cuban trade embargo is now under much closer control by Congress and has become more difficult to modify. Under the Helms-Burton Law United States nationals and corporations may sue foreign companies that are involved in any business venture in Cuba that involves American property confiscated by the Cuban government since the Revolution of 1959. This includes much of the business property in Cuba before 1959. Those who sue need not have been American nationals or corporations at the time the property was confiscated. American presidents do have the power to suspend the right to bring these suits for six-month intervals, and so far they have regularly done so. However, executives of companies engaged in such business practices have been banned from entering the United States, as have foreign products that may have Cuban components.

Also prohibited is trade with Cuba by American companies who use a third party, such as a foreign subsidiary or other foreign company as an intermediary. Canada sees this as an attempt to impose extra-territoriality on its citizens and businesses by applying American law to business activity that take place outside the United States. It recognizes the right of the United States to have whatever internal trade regulations it wishes, but it has gone so far as to pass legislation forbidding Canadians living in Canada from complying with the United States trade embargo and the Helms-Burton law. Cuba is the country's largest Caribbean trading partner. Cuban goods, mostly tobacco products, are readily available in Canadian stores, and Canadians are free to visit Cuba for business or holiday purposes.

The situation reached a low point when in March 2002 James Sabzali, a Canadian citizen living in the United States, became the first foreign national ever convicted of violating the Trading with the Enemy Act. He and the Bala Cynwood, Pennsylvania, company that employed him, along with several of the company's officers, were accused of selling chemical resins used in water purification systems to Cuba through third parties in Canada and Mexico. Canada was angry over the case because many of the alleged sales took place while Sabzali was still living in Canada and up to four years before he moved to Pennsylvania. The Canadian public has strongly supported Sabzali. There is little reason to believe that the Canadian and American governments can resolve their differences over the Helms-Burton legislation as long as the trade embargo remains in effect.

Most serious disputes between the United States and Canada do involve trade matters. Washington accused Canada of unfairly subsidizing and dumping Canadian softwood lumber on the American market and imposed an import tariff in excess of 27 percent on Canadian lumber. The exception to these tariffs was lumber from the Maritime Provinces, which were exempted since their policies were considered legal and proper. Canada denied the charges and felt the tariff was simply to protect American timber companies. Interestingly and logically enough, the Canadians did have a powerful American ally in the construction industry. In 2006 the two countries finally did resolve their differences and reached an agreement on lumber that greatly lowered the tariff.

A seemingly perpetual dispute is that over fishing for Pacific salmon. Not only does it involve the two federal governments but also the provincial government of British Columbia, the state of Alaska, and to a lesser extent Washington and Oregon. A 1985 treaty signed after fifteen years of negotiations was intended to regulate the industry. Under the terms of the Pacific Salmon Treaty neither country was to catch more fish than it produces. The problem is in attempting to set an annual quota for the catches. Salmon return to spawn in the river or stream where they were born. A fish caught off Alaska may have been born there, but possibly its life began in British Columbia. Those catching it may argue it is an "American fish," while others declare in reality it is a "Canadian fish." It is possible to determine to some extent how many fish originating in each country are actually caught by studying the migratory patterns, but the salmon catch is an emotional issue that is not always debated on logical or scientific grounds. At times tempers have flared badly, leading in one instance to Canadian fishermen temporarily preventing an American vessel from leaving the British Columbia port of Prince Rupert, an act which ultimately led to them being fined. Usually things do not go that far, and an agreement is worked out for another fishing season. However, the underlying problems remain, and the fishery continues to be in danger of being depleted.

Wheat sales are another irritant between the two countries. On February 15, 2002, the Washington Office of the United States Trade Representative, responding to a complaint by the North Dakota Wheat Commission, announced it would take steps to combat the trading practices of the Canadian Wheat Board, which it deemed a "government monopoly trading enterprise." The Trade Representative claims the Canadian government permits the Board special monopoly rights and privileges that "give it competitive advantages that hurt U.S. wheat farmers." As we have noted earlier, the Board does control wheat and barley sales for the farmers of Western Canada in order to try to obtain better prices on world markets. Ironically some Canadian grain farmers, who prefer to handle their own sales, would side with the Trade Representative and call for drastic reductions or the complete abolishment of the Wheat Board's powers. Farmers have actually been arrested and fined for illegal grain sales. Prime Minister Stephen Harper's government is proposing that the Wheat Board monopoly at least be reconsidered.

There have been other, if less dramatic arguments, over such things as the importation of Prince Edward Island potatoes. The typical pattern in most of these matters is for the two sides to ultimately quietly negotiate a compromise and resolve the matter, at least for a period of time. This is generally true of even the more serious disagreements. Canadian-American trade is too vital, and the relationship between the two countries too important, to let these things fester. Nevertheless, some, like the salmon fishery, may sorely try the patience of all parties involved.

While hardly the most serious, one of the strangest disputes between the United States and Canada is that over Machias Seal Island. Located southwest of New Brunswick's Grand Manan Island and east of the coast of Maine, this bird sanctuary and nearby waters are claimed by both countries. If possession is "nine-tenths of the law," Canada would seem to have the upper hand, since a Canadian lighthouse is maintained on the island. However, no one wants to get into an ugly feud over this spot on the map. A friendly agreement has been reached. One boatload of tourists departs from New Brunswick to visit each morning. A second boatload leaves from Maine in the afternoon. All mariners benefit from the lighthouse.

Everyone is happy, except the New Brunswick lobstermen. They accuse their counterparts from Maine of setting traps in the disputed waters during the months when the New Brunswick lobster season is closed. In retaliation they did lay traps of their own in the hope of forcing negotiations to resolve the conflict.

Trade disputes, large and small, should not cause us to lose sight of the fact that far more is harmonious in the economic relations between the United States and Canada than is subject to disagreement. Each country has billions of dollars invested in the other. Americans have invested more money in Canada than they have anywhere else other than the United Kingdom. Canadian investment in the United States is greater than that of any states other than Japan, the United Kingdom, and the Netherlands. The volume of goods, services, and income between the two countries continues to be the greatest two-way trade relationship to be found anywhere. NAFTA has drastically reduced or entirely eliminated tariffs on goods originating in the United States, Canada, and Mexico that are imported by any one of the three.

In addition to trade differences, Canadians as a whole tend to have a love/hate response to American culture. In the early 1980s remote Northern communities constructed usually unlicensed satellite receiving facilities to rebroadcast American television programs for local residents who were not satisfied with the limited variety provided by the Canadian networks. American books, newspapers, and magazines are widely available, and read throughout the country. A few Canadians seriously advocate a kind of "North American euro" and would do away with their own national currency.

At the same time widespread fear exists that the unique, fragile Canadian culture is under attack and subject to destruction by the domination of American films, television programs, and publications. Canada has countered this perceived threat in a variety of ways. The government generously subsidizes domestic efforts in the fine arts, films, and writing through the Canada Council for the Arts and Telefilm Canada. By law, foreign ownership of Canadian magazines is limited to 49 percent. Foreign magazines without any Canadian editorial content sold in the country may carry no more than 18 percent advertising intended for a Canadian audience.

Private radio and television are abundant, but the government-owned Canadian Broadcasting Corporation is valuable in making available a reliable source for Canadian news and Canadian talent. The CBC also provides specialized programming for French and First Nations audiences. In addition, through the shortwave services of Radio Canada International, along with various television satellite and Internet services, it is able to take the " Canadian message" around the world. Like government agencies in many lands, periodically one service of the CBC or another must do battle against proposed or actual budget cuts, but few would seriously believe or advocate that this powerful voice fall silent. The Canadian Radio-television and Telecommunications Commission (CRTC), which is the regulatory body for nongovernmental radio and television stations, requires radio stations to play at least 35 percent Canadian music. The domestic music industry has benefited as a result.

Canada has come a long way since 1864 when five sparsely populated British colonies, fearing a possible American invasion and hoping to increase trade, came together at Charlottetown, Prince Edward Island, to explore the alleged benefits of union. It is appropriate that the Canadian sociologist Marshall McLuhan, first coined the term "global village," because as communication and transportation grids shrink our planet, Canada seems destined to play an important role in its future. A nation with virtually no enemies, a solid civil rights record, and highly regarded by most of the world, can make a significant contribution to international peace and prosperity. Canada will continue to be a most valuable friend and neighbor to the United States as well. At the same time, no one should forget this is a fully sovereign and independent state. As such she should be expected when possible to work for the common good but not at the expense of neglecting or harming her own interests. The world would do well to hope that Canada continues to raise up wise and capable leaders who will guide her skillfully in the years ahead.

CANADA'S TOMORROWS

A Look at the Possible Future

Trying to read the future with certainty is impossible. Nevertheless, a look at Canada's 2001 census and events since reveal intriguing possibilities. There are strong hints as to where the nation is heading in the years immediately ahead.

Canada's population now exceeds thirty-two million, but the growth rate is slow. This is typical of most developed nations, but Canada could accommodate a higher rate of growth, especially when the aging of her population is taken into account. Today immigration contributes more to growth than natural population increase. Rather than be concerned about immigration, as are some economically developed countries, the Canadian government actually encourages its increase.

Immigration could have some positive effects on Canadian society beyond the expected ones of contributing to the workforce and economic growth. Most of the new arrivals, regardless of what language they speak, are hardly likely to see themselves as English Canadians or French Canadians. They expect to become simply Canadians. As such, they can function as a catalyst to help build a political culture that is distinctly Canadian, with less of the tension between French and English that has been present in the past. At the same time those Canadians who are of French and English heritage, along with the First Nations, can continue to contribute their distinctive cultural ingredients as they have done throughout the country's history. Canada has always welcomed immigration, and today it appears well on the way to being a product of globalization, but one wearing a "Proudly made in Canada" label.

Former Finance Minister and Prime Minister Paul Martin also sees immigration as the critical element in transforming Canada into the first "post-modern country." As such, he thinks it is in the ideal position to be the leader in the age of globalization, particularly when American interests are often focused nationally and European ones regionally.

The 2006 election of the Conservative Party of Canada government under the leadership of Prime Minister Stephen Harper may help to strengthen the ties that bind Canadians together. A son of Alberta, Harper's leadership should considerably lessen the "Western alienation" that sometimes sweeps across the Prairie Provinces. As noted, his government has finally brought a resolution to the long-standing softwood lumber dispute between the United States and Canada.

Among all these positives there are concerns that should not be overlooked. Francophones do fear that immigrants may tend to ignore their language, sensing that learning English is likely to provide more employment opportunities. This could lead to a weakening of the French cultural influence throughout the country and even in Quebec. As in other countries, some Canadians also are concerned about competition for jobs from immigrants.

The nation shows increasing signs of urbanization. Approximately 80 percent of the population lives in urban areas of 10,000 or more. Much of this is concentrated in just four centers. Slightly more than half of all Canadians will be found in the Montreal area, southern Ontario's so called Golden Horseshoe (the west and northwest shores of Lake Ontario), the Calgary-Edmonton corridor, and the Lower Mainland of British Columbia. In these places the suburbs that form a "doughnut" around the central urban cores are growing even faster than the cities themselves. These are the sections of the country that are financially doing especially well, although they are not immune to the normal economic cycles that tend to impact everywhere. There is every reason to believe they will continue to do well in the coming years, and their population gains should also translate into political ones as well.

The rural areas face a more difficult future. This is especially true in Atlantic Canada, which once thrived on the wealth of its forests and fisheries. While they still contribute to the economy, more diversification and growth are needed if the region is to close the gap with the more prosperous parts of the country. Perhaps due to its finally being connected to the mainland through Confederation Bridge, Prince Edward Island has shown a small increase in people between 1996 and 2001. New Brunswick and Nova Scotia experienced small losses, while Newfoundland and Labrador shrunk by 7 percent. A few places did buck the trend. Fredericton, capital of New Brunswick, actually added people, and Nova Scotia had the smallest decline of any province with a population loss. Still, one must conclude that while this region of the country has much to offer in both beauty and tranquility, Canadians and foreign immigrants are discouraged from settling there because employment opportunities are better elsewhere.

It would not be responsible to expect too much too soon, but there are some signs that the Atlantic Provinces and the federal government are making serious efforts to reverse the situation. Further, they appear to be having some success. The agreement between Inco and Newfoundland and Labrador should lead to the creation of thousands of mining jobs in Labrador at Voisey's Bay and eventually positions at the proposed smelter on Newfoundland. The native peoples of Labrador should receive economic benefits as well. The provincial government has also returned to the bargaining table with that of Quebec in the hope that they can reach an accord on a hydroelectric power project on the Lower Falls of the Churchill River at Gull Island in Labrador. Newfoundland plans to avoid the mistakes made in previous negotiations when most of the benefits from the Upper Falls development went to Quebec.

Nova Scotia and Newfoundland and Labrador, with the intervention of the federal government, have resolved their boundary dispute over the waters of the North Atlantic and the Gulf of Saint Lawrence. This should assist them in developing the potentially profitable oil and gas deposits there. Both provinces are already counting on an expansion of drilling activities in their waters. In July 2002 Canadian Superior Energy began new drilling south of Nova Scotia's Sable Island, an area that already has several successful producing projects. Petro-Canada has launched Newfoundland's second oil project, Terra Nova, which follows the highly successful Hibernia. Some believe Terra Nova could launch the Newfoundland economy into the fastest growing in the entire country. One projection claims that in 2007 only Alberta will have greater growth.

While the cod fishery of the Grand Banks is unlikely to see significant recovery in the immediate future, and much of Newfoundland's population loss can be attributed to the fishery's decline, some Newfoundland and Maritime fishermen hang on to their tradition. Shrimp and crabs along with lobsters are making a positive contribution to the economy of all of the region's provinces. Tourism is also growing in a healthy manner. Confederation Bridge eliminates the long ferry delays when departing to or from Prince Edward Island. Nova Scotia is a popular destination for many American travelers, while portions of New Brunswick also have considerable appeal. The film *Titanic* and the fascination with icebergs did boost Newfoundland's tourism, but the province's isolation makes it more challenging to entice visitors to enjoy its splendors.

Atlantic Canada is seeking to attract more industry and service-based businesses. Nova Scotia has taken advantage of its well-educated workforce and, like Ireland and India, become a center for computer data processing. Moncton, New Brunswick, in 2002 made history by becoming the first municipality in the entire country to become officially bilingual. This, along with the fact that New Brunswick is the only province in Canada to be officially bilingual (at the provincial government level), may help create an environment conducive to attracting Canadian companies and even those from elsewhere. Students and young people who have recently entered the workforce will tell you that when looking for employment it pays to be bilingual.

Atlantic Canada is entering a time of major transition. Old resource-based industries have declined, while others have risen to partially take their place. The journey to a more diverse and complex economy is sometimes painful and slow. Still, it progresses, and the final result could ultimately be an economic renaissance.

Quebec is growing slowly, but the province needs more immigration in the face of a low birth rate. For cultural reasons it would love to attract French speakers, and does to some extent. However, most countries with a predominantly French-speaking population are likely to be African (along with Haiti) and have educational levels and technical skills well below what the typical worker needs to be integrated into the Quebec economy. France itself attracts immigrants rather than provides them.

Northern Quebec faces another problem, one it shares with the upper portion of Ontario. Here the economy is resource based and often focused on production of a single commodity. As prices for various metals dropped, some of these communities faced mine closures and population declines. For instance, Schefferville, Quebec, saw most of its inhabitants leave after the closure of its iron mines. Indeed this is a problem throughout the North. When the lead and zinc mine at Nanisivik, on northern Baffin Island in the Nunavut territory, shut down in September 2002, the once thriving community became a ghost town. Some Northern settlements have been able to adjust by diverting their economies to tourism, but for others the days ahead remain very problematic. Increasingly mining companies prefer to fly temporary workers into the mining camps rather than construct complete towns for them. It is possible that the current bull market in commodity prices may revitalize some communities and even attract new residents to them.

Clearly Quebec's future would look brighter if it could resolve the sovereignty issue, and the uncertainty of remaining in or leaving Canada. Some signs point in the direction of a resolution to this question while others do not. Although more pessimistic than their counterparts elsewhere in the country, Quebec residents under age forty tend to be far more optimistic about their future than those over forty. They are more nationalistic than the older generation, but at the same time feel more secure about their place in Canadian society. At least for some, separation may no longer seem to be a necessary step for a successful tomorrow.

Polls in recent years showed support for secession in the neighborhood of 40 percent or slightly higher. This was down considerably from the almost 50 percent who supported it in the 1995 referendum. When asked if they want another vote on the question, an even smaller percentage said yes. Yet another indication that sovereignty might have been losing its allure is the greater visibility of the political party L'Action democratique du Quebec, which can hardly be called federalist but is far more willing to move slowly on the separation issue than Parti Quebecois. Unfortunately for leader Mario Dumont's party, its popularity may ultimately be incompatible with its conservative fiscal and other policies and its hedging on a flat-rate tax proposal. Even former Parti Quebecois Premier Bernard Landry seemed to move in a new direction toward a more accommodating policy, working with the federal government to reach agreements with some of the province's native peoples, a move that was severely criticized by some sovereignists. He also preferred to stress the party's accomplishments rather than sovereignty as he unsuccessfully campaigned for its reelection in the spring of 2003.

On the other hand, it would not be wise to read too much into these factors. Reluctance for another referendum may be more a matter of voter fatigue on this issue rather than a decision to stay. Temporary loss of support for Parti Quebecois and gains for the provincial Liberals led by Jean Charest may have had more to do with issues other than separation. Its decision to merge suburban communities into the city to create one huge Montreal, a mega-city, may have made sense from the standpoint of administrative efficiency and economy, but it was highly unpopular with many who feared loss of community identity. Likewise the party's well intended budget cutting efforts angered civil servants who took the brunt of the cuts and irritated a province which is use to a higher level of social services and benefits than in most of Canada.

Ironically the crisis over Iraq created a resurgence in support for both Parti Quebecois and sovereignty. Francophone Quebecers receive much of their news from France. As a result they were far more likely to oppose American intervention in Iraq than are people in the rest of Canada. This situation has reminded Quebecers that they are different. Thus sovereignty becomes a more logical option than it otherwise might appear. The question of Quebec's future remains perplexing for the entire country. Until Quebec ratifies the Constitution or says goodbye no one can be fully certain about Canada's destiny. However, a November 2006

Parliamentary resolution supported by Prime Minister Stephen Harper and all the major political parties calls for recognition of Quebec as a nation within Canada. While largely symbolic, it just may provide a first step toward a final solution to the question of Quebec's place in the Canadian Confederation.

In the meantime there is much about the Quebec business environment that is healthy and promising. Montreal continues to enjoy a diversified and prosperous economy with even world-class companies such as transportation equipment manufacturer Bombardier headquartered there. The Ottawa Valley communities comprise a sort of Canadian "Silicon Valley" and should remain a technology center in the coming years. Quebec City continues to be a political center and an alluring attraction for both summer and winter tourism. Government-operated Hydro-Quebec is thriving and is essential to power requirements in the United States, such as those of New York, as well as in Canada. The provincial government has reached an agreement with the Cree for further hydroelectric development in the James Bay region and with provisions that will also dramatically improve its relations with First Nations peoples. A similar agreement has also been made with the province's Inuit. These treaties call for aboriginal peoples to actively participate in the development, management, and profits of the hydroelectric, forest, and mineral resources of the North. They could possibly serve as models elsewhere in the country.

Other rural areas seem less bright, but that is true in most regions of Canada. On the whole, the province should have a promising future, one that could make a considerable contribution to Canada should it decide to remain. It is in the best interests of the entire country to take all possible positive steps to encourage it to do so.

The southern Ontario peninsula presently enjoys population growth above the 4.0 percent national average for the past five years. The rate for the entire province was 6.1 percent, and immigration from outside of Canada accounted for a considerable amount of this. Not surprisingly the favorite destinations for immigrants are Toronto and the Golden Horseshoe. This part of the province remains the country's economic heartland with a sophisticated and highly diversified economy. So dynamic is its impact that it probably would be viable as a separate independent state.

Its strength may also be something of a problem. In 1956 Jack McLaren's little book *Let's All Hate Toronto*, ironically published by a Toronto publisher, attracted widespread attention throughout the country. It was a lighthearted, profusely illustrated, piece of satire that its author said was inspired by the animosity he found toward Toronto on the part of Canadians who lived elsewhere. More serious books have also touched on this same theme. Editor Robert Brym's 1986 *Regionalism in Canada* explores the dependency, exploitation, and resentment that the Canadian East and West have sometimes felt toward the country's center. Through programs such as equalization payments to the provinces, the federal government does make more effort than most nations to raise the standard of living in those parts of the country that may lag behind. Along similar lines, in August 2002 Ottawa announced a major financial contribution to help New Brunswick finish widening its portion of the Trans-Canada Highway to four lanes. These policies, and numerous others, are notable, but nevertheless do not change the fact that Canadians in southern Ontario and several other parts of the country do have a higher material standard of living than those residing elsewhere. The task for the nation is of course to preserve and enhance these success stories where they are while at the same time finding creative ways to export them to the rest of the country. Given the success that Ontario should continue to enjoy, the country may indeed have the resources to accomplish this task. Look for this part of Canada to continue to lead.

Manitoba's prairies are seeing slow growth, while those of Saskatchewan are experiencing decline. At first glance the picture may appear more negative than it should. Saskatchewan farms, along with those of Manitoba and Alberta, are consolidating. This actually makes them more efficient producers and cuts the costs of production. Similar changes are taking place in related industries, such as grain storage and hauling. The result of all of this is not a decrease in the value of Prairie agriculture but the need for fewer workers on the land and in the supporting industries. Although Manitoba's rural areas are still seeing some slight growth, most of the population increase on the prairies is in the suburbs surrounding the larger cities. Saskatchewan as a whole may be witnessing little population change but the Regina, Saskatoon, and Winnipeg, Manitoba, metropolitan areas reveal growth. In some ways they show similarities to Toronto, the Ontario Horseshoe, or Montreal. They have strong diversified economies based on a variety of industries and services. As such they are further evidence of the changing nature of the entire Canadian economy in which natural resource industries remain important but no longer play quite as dominant role as they once did.

Temporarily retarding the future of the prairies was the devastating drought that tormented much of the area in recent years. Crop yields were down, and livestock production declined. In some ways this disaster brought out the best in Canadians. Farmers from Ontario, joined by those from British Columbia, Quebec, New Brunswick, and Nova Scotia launched the Hay West campaign to help Prairie farmers feed their livestock. The Canadian Pacific and Canadian National Railways provided free shipping, and the Canadian Armed Forces assisted with logistical advice. In a country noted for its regional distinctions here was a splendid display of the underlying unity that is stronger than many realize and that does bind the country together. Conditions are now considerably better. Prairie agriculture will recover. It survived the dark days of the Depression and the Dust Bowl. This region has many courageous people with a great deal to contribute to Canada's future.

Currently Alberta is booming. The dynamic economy based on petroleum and natural gas, but also supported by tourism and a variety of industries, is responsible for a population increase of 10.3 percent in just five years, by far the highest of any province. Much of this is domestic immigration, especially from Atlantic Canada. On a trip to Calgary a few years ago I discovered my taxi driver was from Newfoundland. While in St. John's, Newfoundland, one man who did have a secure career told me his brother had not been so fortunate and had moved to Alberta where he was happily employed as a carpenter. Housing prices in Calgary have risen, and demand has been steady, even if the market is now cooling to some degree . The entire corridor from Calgary to Edmonton is prospering. Perhaps the Calgary Tower, the city's annual Stampede, which rightly claims to be the world's largest rodeo, and the West

Edmonton Mall are all appropriate symbols of the wealth, growth, and optimism of the area.

Success, possibly along with some American immigration, has produced a more individualistic citizen than the typical Canadian. Albertans work hard, seek their own future, and sometimes feel they are called upon to pay too much of the entire country's bills while not receiving their rightful share of the political power. They have done so well that they have even created a Heritage Fund for the province and use this to help support projects and programs that are of particular interest to them. All is not perfect. Some Albertans believe the province could and should spend more on education and health care. It took the lead in balancing governmental budgets, but may need to review the impact this has had on social welfare. On the whole, however, the coming years ahead should look bright for the province and its increasing number of citizens.

I heard one successful Albertan remark he felt more at home in California than he did in Ottawa. Here is the challenge for all of Canada. The country absolutely needs the wealth and the optimistic approach that Albertans bring to the future. The task is to make them feel that they have more of a stake in what takes place outside Alberta's borders than they think they do now. Among other things, this most likely would require political changes, such as reform of the Senate. However, some of the things that Alberta wants and expects are really things that many other Canadians would also find desirable. The challenge is an attainable one.

Back in the 1980s and early 1990s British Colombia was growing even more rapidly than Alberta is presently. The decline of natural resource prices hurt some of the province's industries, and more recently the American tariff on softwood lumber added to the pain. As a result growth between 1996 and 2001 slowed to 4.9 percent, still higher than the national average but less than that of Alberta or Ontario. The lower mainland continues to see healthy progress. Vancouver is the country's third largest city and its chief Pacific Rim port. It has a reputation for cultural diversity, beauty, and economic muscle. Although growth on the southern part of Vancouver Island, home of the provincial capital, Victoria, is much slower, the relatively mild climate should continue to make this a popular destination for the increasing number of Canadians in their retirement years. The scenic wonder of the province will make it a popular tourist destination and an enchanting place to live.

One matter that the province must resolve is the future of its native peoples. British Columbia has entered into few agreements with Indian bands, and is still debating what form these agreements should take. Canada as a whole is rethinking its nineteenth century Indian Act that forms the basis for relations between First Nations peoples and the federal government. Other provinces are making progress on aboriginal government, and the federal territory of Nunavut has been created for the Inuit. Native peoples are making advances. New Brunswick has discussed the possibility of creating a native peoples riding for voting in Parliamentary elections. British Columbia has the opportunity to learn from these efforts and even improve on them.

Like Alaska, British Columbia also attracts those who love a beautiful land and one that offers them enough space to be as individualistic as they desire. Whether they are among these who want to march to the beat of their own drummer or the more typical urban dweller, British Columbians share to some extent the same concerns that Alberta has. They have much to contribute. They want to feel that as they make that contribution they are truly one with the nation.

An increase in the Inuit birth rate resulted in a population gain for Nunavut of over 8 percent, but this was a total of only two thousand people. Its territorial capital, Iqaluit, grew by 24 percent. The Yukon and Northwest Territories lost population at about the same rate that Nunavut grew, but due to the small populations in the North, the figures tend to be somewhat misleading. In the case of all three territories economic opportunities would appear to be based on natural resources. As we have noted, the Northwest Territories is now a diamond producer, and production should increase in the future. The Yukon and especially the Northwest Territories should benefit from one or possibly two natural gas pipelines proposed to run from Alaska, through Canada, and all the way to the lower states. Native peoples should share in the jobs and royalties these would provide, and the Mackenzie Valley of the Northwest Territories would have a way to transport its natural gas to the lucrative American market. Recent emerald finds in the Yukon raise other interesting possibilities.

As a primarily Inuit territory, Nunavut is making the bold statement that native peoples can successfully govern themselves and their resources and do it while enhancing their culture rather than destroying it. At the same time Nunavut must continue to deal with the challenge of assisting the Inuit as they make the inevitable transition from a completely traditional society to one that is at least partially integrated into the rest of the country and even the world. As tourism increases in the territory, along with the demand for the work of its artists, there is reason to hope this will be successfully accomplished, thus strengthening the appreciation for the culture of these residents of the Far North.

Because Canada is such a diversified country, it is good to look at its prospects on a regional basis, but we must remember the regions comprise one country. That nation should have a dynamic future ahead of it. When we entered the new millennium the Canadian economy, like nearly every other one, showed signs of strain. It also revealed signs of strength and resiliency that will serve it well as it now goes forward again. The nation remains a place of hope and opportunity for immigrants and its young people not only because of its vital economy but because this is still a land of tolerance and compassion.

Look for the Canada of tomorrow to play a major role on the economic stage, but also in international peacekeeping and the struggle for human rights. She will find her own path, one that is truly hers and not that of any other nation, because though she is rightfully proud of her heritage, she is unique and not like any other land. Her path is sure, and her footing is certain.

EPILOGUE
Tides Along the Shore

The previous chapter was intended to be this book's conclusion. However, a recent journey to the New Brunswick coast of the Bay of Fundy suggested an epilogue.

In the course of a normal lifetime all of us visit numerous places. Most are probably ordinary and soon slip out of our memories, perhaps to be occasionally recalled at some future time. A few are special for one reason or another. They are associated with life's passages and its challenges. Others recall great beauty and happiness, and sometimes the inevitable tragedy in human experience. There are also those priceless moments, those times and places that penetrate to the depth of our soul, and, if we have the courage to look inwardly, reveal who we truly are and our ultimate destiny. They are very personal possessions, highly subjective and only partially capable of being understood or shared with another, if we care to share them at all. They have a strange, haunting power to shape and mold us, and strengthen us to continue the journey even on those days when we would just as soon stop and rest for a while.

For me such times and places have almost always been associated with the sea. As a boy my fondest memories were summers spent on the New Jersey shore at Long Beach Island. Anchored on the north end by the historic Barnegat Lighthouse and on the south by a small wildlife sanctuary, the island offered eighteen miles of beach to explore and unconsciously discover who I was and what was important to me. I remember one day, when no more than twelve or thirteen, coming across a tiny forsaken cemetery hidden in some deep dunes and heavy growth. Only a few crumbling markers remained to identify the graves of the nearly forgotten rugged Norwegian fishermen who with their strength, determination, and courage somehow managed to survive and wrest a living out of these waters. It seemed to be sacred ground, made holy by seafarers who asked little from life and gave it all they had to give. Somehow the sea seems to have that power to transform, to make us stronger than we are or ever thought we could be. The young boy stood silent that day, in a sense of awe of these who had journeyed before him and in some unspoken way told him to never give up, no matter the cost.

I would occasionally look for that place again, once even taking my younger sister along to help, but I never could find even a trace of it. The sea gives only in its own time and its own way. Perhaps one look was considered sufficient. Maybe the dunes reclaimed what they had briefly, possibly reluctantly, revealed.

Another time, on a different part of the island I found what appeared to be a giant tooth, washed up on the beach. I felt that whatever creature had surrendered this to the sea may have done so quite willingly, as it appeared to have a huge cavity as much as two inches long. The entire tooth may have been as big as four or five inches. This might have been quite a prize, but for reasons I never understood I permitted a friend who was with me that day to keep it. What he did with it I do not know, and I no longer even know where he is. However, even then I realized the tooth itself was not the important thing. What was important was the mystery it symbolized. Who was the unknown leviathan of this underworld, the former proud owner who used it while plunging the fountains of the deep? The sea is filled with unanswered questions even when seeming to reveal a few of its secrets. It teaches those who care to listen that sometimes the answer is there really is no answer, at least for now. The destination may ultimately be important, but so is the journey. Do not lose sight of it.

Of course spend much time learning from the sea and you become deeply aware of the tides. Possibly the tides are the sea's greatest teachers, for they quietly command and gently but firmly reveal who is ultimately in control. They lead, and they take no orders. They come and go as they please, inviting those who will follow to come along and understand while promptly abandoning those who insist they will be in charge. High tides can thrill with their power and may occasionally delight with the construction of a gully ideal for splashing. Low tides leave behind exotic sea debris and can create long, gentle breakers that ride you safely to shore. Once at a friend's summer home on Topsail Island, North Carolina, I became fascinated observing the family's tidal clock. The tides have a rhythm all their own. Follow it and you will know the best times for body surfing or whatever it is the sea calls you to do. Ignore it, and you may have a few unpleasant surprises.

So what does all this have to do with a book about Canada? The Bay of Fundy creates some of the greatest tidal differences anywhere in the world. There are good scientific explanations for this, and they are not difficult to find, but this is not the place for them. All we need say here is the tides are essentially the result of the length and the narrow width of the Bay. At certain times of the year, particularly the spring and the fall, they may be particularly strong, but their presence is evident in any season. Travel coastal New Brunswick, the Fundy Trail, and the tides will soon be your guide. They will unfold wonders of nature and scenes of great beauty, but they will also point to things deeper. You will come to understand the hold this sometimes harsh but beautiful land can have on people. Some leave for places where living is easier, but others do stay. Like the tides this is their home, and they learn to live with it no matter the price.

I had gone to the Fundy coast actually to do some research on Canada's past and present situation. My efforts were successful, but in the end it was the tides that claimed my soul. If you have read this far perhaps you see why. If you do not, well please go along for the rest of the journey and experience this world where one learns to live by a different time and where silence is often the loudest teacher. Undoubtedly the Nova Scotia Fundy coast has its own treasures to reveal, but my sojourn was confined to the New Brunswick shore. Nova Scotia will have to be reserved for a future day.

Saint John: The Reversing Falls

West of New Brunswick's largest city, Saint John, the coast along the Bay of Fundy offers some enticing attractions. St. Andrews is a lovely old town, filled with historical sites, a vintage hotel, quaint shops, and a botanical garden. Nearby St. Stephen is home to a fascinating chocolate museum and factory store. A modest detour through Maine will ultimately take you back into New Brunswick and Campobello Island, the summer home of Franklin Roosevelt's family. There are other worthwhile stops as well, but it is the area from Saint John eastward where I found those Fundy tides play their most mystical games, and so it is to there we must now venture.

Despite the intrusion of a paper pulp mill upon the setting, the Reversing Falls at Saint John (never abbreviated to St. John nor to be confused with Newfoundland's St. John's) have the power to hold in a hypnotic spell. Here the Saint John River meets the Bay of Fundy, and each is determined to be the winner in this perpetual struggle. At low tide the salt waters of the bay retreat into the harbor, and for now the river has the upper hand as it spills over the rocks, creating wild and beautiful rapids and whirlpools on its way to the sea. Victory is only temporary. Gradually the churning of the waters diminishes.

At slack tide Nature declares a tie. The river and the bay form a brief and uneasy truce. At this time there are no traces of the rocks or rapids in the river. The surface is as calm as a lake, and boats can easily pass under the bridge that spans the bluffs on both sides of the falls and continue up the river. However, they must not tarry. After approximately twenty minutes the waters begin to stir again, gradually at first and then slowly with more force. Now it is the tide and the bay that are winning. Salt water flows over the rocks pushing the river water back as the falls reverse. Where the salt and fresh water meet, a flock of birds greets them. Fish swimming in with the tide reach the fresh water, do not like it, and seek to retreat. It is at this moment that they are vulnerable to the hungry winged creatures who are wise to these strange doings of Nature. Eventually the cycle begins to repeat itself, with the tide gradually losing its strength, retreating to slack tide and the temporary return of still waters.

You can watch this ever-changing spectacle from several vantage points near the falls or through the widows of a conveniently located restaurant. In the summer you can even ride a speedboat over the rapids and through the eddies, if you are willing to get rather wet. No matter how you experience the falls they are a perpetual reminder that things are always in flux, ever changing, and yet there is a sameness, a continuity, about them. When we think we know exactly where we are going maybe we really do not. When we believe nothing around us seems to make any sense, we may have stumbled upon the key that makes sense of everything. The falls have much wisdom to impart to those willing to go with the flow, yet capable of changing direction when the time is ripe.

St. Martins: The Sea Caves

The village of St. Martins lies east of Saint John, about one hour's drive on the Fundy Trail. It is a serene little community that makes one wish to stay and linger awhile. If you are inclined to do so, there are several establishments that can accommodate visitors. East of town the road tantalizes with one of those places that haunt the pages of every tourist brochure yet too often seem to be an illusion when you actually get there. This one is real enough. A modest harbor accommodates several fishing boats along with small buildings for stowing equipment and supplies. Across the street is a small, picturesque lighthouse that serves as a visitors' center. Between the lighthouse and the harbor, the road once again delights as it transverses the Vaughan Creek Covered Bridge. This is actually a double bridge, with a smaller roofed passage for pedestrian traffic along side the larger one for vehicles. Rounding a bluff, there is a broad open view of the Bay of Fundy, and a magnificent first sighting of the two sea caves. Carved by the incredible tides out of the soft reddish-brown, sandstone rock, they have a forbidding air about them.

At low tide a wide rock-covered beach makes access to the caves possible.

We carefully made our way over the difficult footing. Some kind but unknown explorer had constructed a crude little footbridge out of two boards and several stones. It provided a precarious passage over a persistent stream that crossed the beach on its way to the bay. We made our way carefully across the bridge and the rest of the beach to finally reach our goal. One cave resembles a large wedge cut into the rock, but the other is a true cavern, with a roof overhead. This one yielded a memorable window to the world outside its entrance. From inside a sea cave the places you just left have an almost mystical beauty about them. Both caves were filled with various wonders, strangely shaped pieces of driftwood and other souvenirs of the deep.

Inside the caves the imagination can hear the waves, perhaps at high tide during a winter storm pounding into the walls, making a strange sort of music all their own. Indeed this is the secret of the power of the tides. The rock appears firm and unyielding. The tides come and go, leaving things much as they were before. Slowly the persistence of the tides wins out, and the rocks must yield. The tides will run the race until the course is finished no matter how long it takes. They will overcome the seemingly impenetrable obstacle they encounter. They will achieve their goal.

Cape Enrage: On a Clear Day You Can See Forever

Fundy National Park is a popular destination for visitors to Canada's Maritime Provinces because it possesses a memorable beauty and serenity. Situated on the Bay of Fundy where it narrows further to become Chignecto Bay, it offers pleasant views of the Nova Scotia coast, along with numerous trails to explore. One descends into a deep, lush ravine to the impressive Dickson Falls. Others, such as Shiphaven and Point Wolfe, furnish easy access to the peaceful shoreline and opportunities to observe the fascinating Fundy tides. For those desiring something longer and more challenging there are plenty of additional trails. After seeing the park, continue eastward for a destination fewer travelers are likely to reach. That is unfortunate, because it really should not be missed.

The roads to Cape Enrage are only for the wide-awake and very sober. Even then I do not think I would want to drive them in bad weather. Twisting, winding and heavily patched they force the driver to pay attention, except when one is wondering if the effort to get there is really worth it. Actually, it is. High on a bluff sits the little Cape Enrage lighthouse and what is possibly the most magnificent view along the entire Fundy coast. The lighthouse and grounds have been lovingly restored and maintained by high school students from Moncton. There is also a small gift shop and in the summer months a restaurant in the restored keeper's house. Beyond these few, harmonious human additions there are only the untamed allure and power of the Fundy shore. At low tide an extensive stone-covered beach is visible. At high tide it is under water, and you may be able to see the force of the tides as they rise and fall creating strong currents around any rocks visible above the waterline.

This place does not let go. Part of me desires to be here during a wild, winter storm. Another part would wish to be as far away as possible during such a time. One thing is certain. Cape Enrage is a free spirit. It will share what it has to offer, but it values its freedom too much to ever permit you to control it, no matter what price you may be willing to offer. You leave here knowing that somehow that is the way it should and must be. Some things help save civilization by refusing to be a part of it. So it is with Cape Enrage.

Hopewell Rocks: The Photograph Becomes Reality

One of the most photographed spots in New Brunswick is the Hopewell Rocks at Hopewell Cape on Shepody Bay, an even further narrowing of Chignecto Bay. The rocks are often featured on promotional tourist literature. It is not difficult to understand why. They are oddities of nature, creations that one thinks should not exist, yet, there they are. They are the creations of the Fundy tides.

The most visited and the most photographed are the Flowerpot Rocks. These are huge pillars of soft dark stone that have been sculpted by the tidal waters. Generally each has a broad base, then a narrow column, and is completed with a somewhat wider and longer section of rock. On the top of most there is an intriguing covering of live trees and various shrubs, brave enough to cling to this precarious perch. It is this crown that is responsible for the flowerpot name. At high tide it is possible to kayak among the rocks, but they are best appreciated at low tide when you can walk the beach, stand beside them, and marvel at both their shape and size. Two of the structures are so close together they form a kind of natural tunnel, making it possible to use them as some sort of gateway into this enchanted world. They are indeed a wonder, and it is not surprising that the Hopewell Rocks receive a significant number of visitors each summer.

Ironically it is the creation of these oddities that ultimately leads to their destruction. The tides continue their work, slowly but constantly, cutting into the rock. Eventually the narrow middle of the rock column collapses, the pillar falls, and the "flowerpot" is smashed to pieces. Evidence of this is easily spotted on the beach where huge slabs of stone provide testimony to the mortality of past creations. Yet, in the midst of destruction there is also creation. As old pots are being undermined, the tides cut into cliffs, carving out grottos that ultimately in their own time will become new flowerpots. The process is slow, but it is also relentless. The tides seem to sense that life and death are part of the natural cycle. Each comes in its own appointed time, and each is dependent on the other. They are ultimately one and the same. At birth we slowly begin the journey toward death. Perhaps at death we begin the journey toward life.

Moncton: The Tidal Bore

North of Hopewell Cape, on the Petitcodiac River, which flows into Shepody Bay, is the pleasant city of Moncton. It can boast a dual nature, having served as an early home for British Loyalists, who had no desire to rebel against king or motherland during the American Revolution, and for French Acadians, who wished only to stay out of both British and French political quarrels and work their lands in peace. Moncton possesses an excellent Acadian Museum, located on the campus of the French-speaking University of Moncton. It is well worth a visit. However, it may be better known for two oddities of nature, Magnetic Hill, and the famous tidal bore.

Magnetic Hill is a delightful optical illusion. Your car appears to roll uphill. Similar experiences can be had elsewhere, including Lake Wales, Florida's, Spook Hill, but the effect at Magnetic Hill is quite dramatic and worth enjoying.

Do not to miss the tidal bore. There are very few places on the entire planet where it occurs. Moncton, and several nearby towns on the Petitcodiac, is on that select list. Old timers remember the tidal bores of another era. A wall of water, several feet high, and accompanied by flocks of birds, would come roaring up the river from the Bay of Fundy covering the exposed mud flats of the river bottom while announcing in this unique manner that high tide was on its way. The bore still arrives at Moncton one hour and thirty-eight minutes before high tide. This provides two chances a day to see it, but delay your arrival, and you will have to wait half a day for another opportunity. Nature keeps her own schedule. The best viewing spots are Bore Park in downtown Moncton, where the viewing time is conveniently posted, or nearby Settlers' Landing, which provides a somewhat closer but shorter look.

Unfortunately bore watchers today will not witness what the old timers did. No one is certain what causes the tidal bore, but there is general agreement that the waters of the Petitcodiac River flowing south and meeting powerful Fundy tides making their way up the riverbed have something to do with it. Wind also can add to the height of the bore. Sadly the Petitcodiac can no longer supply the abundant source of water it once provided. Moncton and Riverview, on the south side of the river, are joined by a narrow two-lane bridge, inadequate for today's traffic needs. Some years ago, further west, a causeway was constructed to carry a new highway that now connects the two communities more conveniently and safely. The price paid for this is that the causeway acts as a dam, dramatically limiting the flow of river water to the bay. This appears to have also contributed to the silting of the river mouth, partially obstructing the passage of the tides northward.

Today in the spring and fall you may see a tidal bore of as much as one foot making its way up the river at modest speed. If you dare to brave a wild and windy storm it might be even higher. In the summer the bore often is more of a ripple, diminishing to as little as two inches. In any case, the bore must die when it reaches the causeway.

We were fortunate enough to see the tidal bore one late spring day when it was about ten inches high. Though a shadow of its former self, it still put on quite a performance while progressing on its journey and, as in the past, accompanied by a supporting cast of many birds. This was a beautiful sight. It was also a sad one. Nature had been violated. When that happens sooner or later she makes humans pay the price. The tides of Fundy have many valuable lessons to teach. One of the most important is that we are stewards of this world, not its masters. We share the planet with many other species also dependent on it, and we are entrusted to pass it on to future generations in good condition. Forget that and the damage at first may seem minimal. Over time it will add up and accelerate at an alarming geometric rate.

The journey ultimately must come to an end. Maybe it is most appropriate that this one end on the shores of the Bay of Fundy, a much loved Canadian possession, and a fitting symbol for an entire country filled with treasures too often over looked or not understood by outsiders. Should this exploration of Canada have encouraged you to visit, you will find its people warm on even the coldest days. From British Columbia to Newfoundland, and Pelee Island to Ellesmere Island, it contains an almost unbelievable variety of landscapes, cultures, and heritage, which come together to create a civil society that is unique and precious. This is the Canada I have come to know, and to love.

APPENDIX I
Immigrating to Canada

Americans are a people proud of their own country, and they often see it as a land offering great opportunities. They do not usually think about immigrating to another nation. Nevertheless around the world, and in every country, there are inevitably some who wonder about what life would be like somewhere else. Not surprisingly, Canada may be one of the places that gains their curiosity.

In recent years interest in immigrating to Canada has greatly increased. The country's attractiveness is hardly surprising. With a vast land area and approximately 32,000,000 people, Canada has long encouraged immigration and continues to do so. Its high standard of living and tolerant, democratic political environment also make it a place that appeals to many. Also its growing economic strength has provided additional opportunities for persons who have the skills Canadian business and industry need.

Those seriously investigating the possibility of living in Canada either permanently or on a temporary basis should visit Citizenship and Immigration Canada's excellent web site (http://www.cig.gc.ca). There you will find all the information you need along with forms that can be downloaded to apply for the necessary immigration visa. Americans do not need a visa for tourism, but everyone does who plans to live there.

Since legal requirements do change from time to time, exploring the web site is essential for anyone seriously considering immigration. We can offer here a few general insights that may prove helpful before looking deeper. Canada does have special programs for the reunification of families, those who may qualify as refugees, and students wishing to study in the country. Again, information on these is offered on the web site.

In its regular immigration programs, like virtually every other country, Canada wants to admit only those persons who have a high probability of successful settlement and have something to contribute to the good of the nation. Immigrants should normally be able to prove they have sufficient funds to take care of themselves and any accompanying family members for up to six months. They must also be free of a criminal record. In very rare instances exceptions might be made, but it would not be wise to count on this. You also need to be able to prove you are in good health and to furnish a list of the household and personal items you wish to bring with you.

Persons are usually admitted as skilled workers, business class immigrants, or provincial nominees. With the exception of Ontario, every province, along with the Yukon Territory, maintains a program to attract immigrants they feel would bring something helpful to their part of Canada. The province of Quebec sponsors a special program for immigrants who are particularly suited for living there. Links to all the provincial immigration programs can be found at the Citizenship and Immigration web site.

You can take a sample test on the web to see if you would probably qualify to enter as a skilled worker. Generally you will be scored on your proficiency in either English or French, education, work experience, age, and whether or not you may have any prearranged employment.

Business class immigrants fall into three categories. Investors must have a net worth of at least CDN$800,000 and be prepared to invest at least CDN$400,000. Entrepreneurs should possess at least CDN$300,000. Self-employed persons must be able to manage a farm or to make a significant contribution to the country's cultural or athletic life.

Those seeking Canadian citizenship, regardless of their original entry status, must meet certain general requirements. They should be at least eighteen years of age, although parents can apply on behalf of their children. Applicants must be permanent residents and have been in Canada three of the four years before they apply. It may be possible to count previous time in Canada toward the three-year residency requirement. Future citizens must be able to use either English or French, know the basic facts about Canada, and understand the rights and responsibilities of Canadian citizenship. Dual citizenship may be possible to maintain, but this should be explored very carefully before any decision is made about applying for Canadian citizenship.

Today Canada is a beacon of opportunity for persons from all parts of the world. It is truly multicultural. Those who have chosen to come here and make it their home have helped to create a nation that is unique and vibrant. Immigrants should continue to help build Canada long into the future.

APPENDIX II

Internet Resources

In this section you will find a variety of Internet web sites that should prove useful in obtaining information on almost any general subject pertaining to Canada. Obviously given the seemingly infinite number of World Wide Web sites, only a small selection can be included. If you are searching for something you want to find, a good search engine such as Google, Yahoo, or Lycos should help you locate it with almost no trouble. For example, if you are looking for Inuit art, any of these portals will take you to a variety of museums that display it and a generous selection of galleries that sell it. Simpatico/MSN is a particularly helpful search engine (http://simpatico.msn.ca). Based in Canada, it has a filter that enables you to filter out non-Canadian sites, if you wish. In addition to its search capabilities, it also provides other basic information. Another similar site with ability to search only Canadian sources if you desire is Canadaspace (http://www.canadaspace.com). With just a few exceptions, web sites indicated throughout the book are not included here. Those that are listed usually link with numerous others, making them quite useful and flexible.

Most Canadian sites are available in either English or French, and occasionally other languages as well. If you want to practice that high school French you took some years ago, they can provide a pleasant way to do so!

Sites with a Wide Variety of Information

(1) Canadiana: The Canadian Resource Page

http://www.cs.cmu.edu/Unofficial/Canadiana/README.html

This is one of the most interesting and useful sites available. It provides travel, financial, and other helpful information and links with all kinds of sources both serious and not so serious.

(2) Government of Canada Primary Internet Site

http://canada.gc.ca

A source for business and travel information, foreign policy, the arts, culture, history, recreational activities, information for non-Canadians, and much more.

Canadian Government Sites

(1) Canadian Embassy in Washington

http://www.canadianembassy.org

A good news source, with convenient links to provincial and territorial tourist offices.

(2) Government Information Branch

http://www.communication.gc.ca/index_e.html

Canadian facts, services guide, surveys, publications from the Department of Public Works and Government Service

(3) Department of Foreign Affairs and International Trade

http://www.dfait-maeci.gc.ca

Good source for economic and travel information.

(4) Elections Canada

http://www.elections.ca

Provides a wealth of federal electoral data.

(5) Parliament of Canada

http://www.parl.gc.ca

(6) Prime Minister's Office

http://pm.gc.ca

Provides news, information on the government, and a variety of general information.

(7) Statistics Canada

http://www.statcan.ca

The source for statistical data on just about everything Canadian

(8) Supreme Court of Canada

http://www.scc-csc.gc.ca

Links to the Court's online library catalog.

Other Government Sources

(1) Nunavut

Department of Indian and Northern Affairs Canada

http://www.inac.gc.ca

Information on Inuit and all First Nations affairs.

Nunavut Planning Commission

http://www.npc.nunavut.ca

News, maps, information on the Inuit Land Claims Agreement.

(2) Provincial and Territorial Governments

http://canada.gc.ca/othergov/prov_e.html

Links with provincial and territorial sites. Useful for tourist information.

(3) Quebec government portal

http://www.gouv.qc/Index_en.html

Provides tourist and general information in both French and English. Links with Quebec regional sites, which may be available only in French.

Media and Related Sources

(1) Canadian Broadcasting Corporation (CBC)

http://www.cbc.ca

Links with radio and television. Provides live audio as well as text.

(2) Macleans

http://www.macleans.ca

Macleans is one of Canada's best known and respected periodicals.

(3) National Library of Canada

http://www.nlc-bnc.ca/index-e.html

A good source for information on both the federal and provincial governments. Links with the Canadian National Archives.

(4) Newspapers and Related

Canada.com Network

http://www.canada.com

Links with the *National Post*. National and regional news, sports, finances.

The Globe and Mail

http://www.theglobeandmail.com

National Post

http://www.canada.com/nationalpost/index.html

Links with the *Financial Post*.

Many local Canadian daily newspapers have their own web sites. Use any major search engine to find them

(5) Canada West Foundation

http://cwf.ca

Provides a variety of information on the interests and views of Western Canada.

(6) *Canada Calling*

http://www.canadacalling.com

This radio program has been on the air for over fifty years. Popular host Prior Smith broadcasts from November to April to Canadians spending the winter in Florida, the Bahamas, South Texas, and Arizona. He is always delighted to also have American listeners to his informative show. The web site provides a list of stations carrying the program and the times it can be heard.

Other Sources

(1) Canadian Football League(CFL)

http://www.cfl.ca

Links to individual team sites and with the useful, general information provider Canoe.

http://www.cflpa.com

Site of the CFL Players' Association.

(2) Canadian Tourism Commission

http://www.travelcanada.ca

Weather, currency, virtual tours, legal essentials, and more.

(3) Early Canadiana Online

http://www.canadiana.org/eco/index.html

Excellent source for historical documents pertaining to Canada. Limited free access for nonmembers.

America On Line

AOL users have access to a wealth of Canadian information. In the keyword box type the following: (Canada.aol.com). This will take you to AOL Canada. Here you will be able to explore and access a wide variety of material about all aspects of Canada.

APPENDIX III

Internet Sources for Canadian Financial Information

Below are some links that may prove useful for those who desire more information on the Canadian economy and financial matters. All have free information available. Some may charge for portions of the content they provide. We cannot vouch for the accuracy or reliability of any of the information furnished. The providers are solely responsible for the content.

I. *Agricultural Commodities*

Winnipeg Commodity Exchange: This is the country's largest commodity exchange and a major market for wheat and other grains.

http://www.wce.ca

Canadian Wheat Board: This is a Crown or government corporation, which has responsibility for the marketing of most of the wheat and barley crop. The present Conservative government is considering some possible changes in its current status.

http://www.cwb.ca/public/en/

Potato Board: An interesting site providing information on the Prince Edward Island potato crop.

http://www.peipotato.org

II. The Stock Exchanges

Toronto Stock Exchange: This is the country's major stock exchange and the place where most large and mid-size Canadian corporations are listed. The site is a useful place to start researching companies and to obtain free quotations of listed companies.

http://www.tsx.com

TSX Venture Exchange, previously known as the Canadian Venture Exchange: The place to find most junior or smaller companies as well as many newer ones. It is owned by the Toronto Stock Exchange but operates as a separate entity.

http://www.tsx.com

Montreal Stock Exchange: The country's oldest stock exchange and the center for much of the Canadian derivatives market. It continues to list many junior Quebec-based companies, while using the facilities of the Canadian Venture Exchange for the actual trading of these.

http://www.m-x.ca/accueil_fr.php

III. Media Sources of Information

Financial Post: This might be called the Canadian *Wall Street Journal*. It provides very thorough coverage of Canada's financial situation. The regular weekly edition is often sold where Canadian newspapers are sold. A limited amount of material can be found by going to the *National Post* web site, which links with it.

http://www.canada.com/nationalpost/index.html

Toronto *Globe and* Mail: Probably the country's best know newspaper, it has excellent financial coverage.

http://www.theglobeandmail.com

Canada Newswire: This site can furnish Canadian company "snapshots" and permits searches for information by date.

http://www.newswire.ca/en/

Canada Stockwatch: Operating out of Vancouver, this site offers some free as well as subscriber material on stocks, recent trades, and articles.

http://www.stockwatch.com

Canoe: Excellent source for regional Canadian news and has a good money section offering stock quotes.

http://www.canoe.ca/Canoe/Classic/home.html

MPL Communications: Produces several quality financial publications.

http://www.adviceforinvestors.com

Sympatico/MSN Canada: This includes a Finance Section, Canadian and other news.

http://sympatico.msn.ca

Yahoo: Yahoo maintains a good Canadian news service that includes a special business section.

http://ca.news.yahoo.com

IV. Other Resources

Chapters-Indigo: This is Canada's largest book retailer. The result of a merger of two companies, you will find its stores throughout the country. They are always worth a visit. Both its retail outlets and its web sites are excellent places to look for books dealing with Canadian financial matters or anything else pertaining to the country.

http://www.chapters.indigo.ca

APPENDIX IV
Suggestions for Further Reading

The titles listed below are not intended to be some sort of list of definitive books on Canada or any particular aspect of Canadian society. They simply constitute books I have encountered over the years and found enjoyable and useful. Hopefully some may appeal to you as well. The editions listed are the ones I have found, but in some cases you may find earlier or later ones. I make no apology for the substantial number of mostly photographic collections. They are my way of bringing a little of Canada home with me.

Many of these books may be out of print. With the help of the Internet, probably most can be found, and you can research for additional ones as well. Amazon (http://www.amazon.com) and Barnes & Noble (http://www.barnesandnoble.com) are two good possibilities. Do not overlook Canadian sources, including Chapters-Indigo (http://www.chapters.indigo.ca) and Abebooks (http://www.abebooks.com). They are happy to serve American customers. In addition your local booksellers may have additional contacts and be able to uncover that elusive title for you.

Barrett, Wayne, and Edith Robinson. *Prince Edward Island.* Halifax: Nimbus Publishing Limited, 1990.
Photographs of Canada's smallest and very picturesque province.

Bell, David V. J. *The Roots of Disunity: A Study of Canadian Political Culture.* 2nd edition. Toronto: Oxford University Press, 1992.
A scholarly and very readable treatment of Canadian political culture, regionalism, and the differences between French and English Canada.

Berton, Pierre. *Why We Act Like Canadians: A personal exploration of our national character.* Markham, Ontario: Penguin Books Canada, 1987.
Berton skillfully explains the major differences between Canadians and Americans.

Bickle, Ian. *Turmoil and Triumph: The Controversial Railway to Hudson Bay.* Calgary: Detselig Enterprises Limited, 1995.
The story of the heroic construction of the still-functioning railway to Churchill, Manitoba.

Bienvenue a Saint-Boniface, Manitoba. Winnipeg: La Societe historique de Saint-Boniface and Le Musee de Saint Boniface, 1991.
This history of the Metis and French community of Saint Boniface, now part of Winnipeg, was issued in connection with a 1991-1993 traveling exhibit of the city's history from its beginnings to 1914. Text in English and French. Difficult to locate.

Blake, Max. *Why Labrador Will Separate from Newfoundland.* Privately published by the author, 1997.
The case for Labrador separatism told by a separatist. Difficult to locate.

Blake, Raymond R. *Canadians at Last: Canada Integrates Newfoundland as a Province.* Toronto: University of Toronto Press, 1994.
The story of the creation of Canada's last and somewhat reluctant province.

Bradley, Michael, with Deanna Theilman-Bean. *Holy Grail Across the Atlantic. The Secret History of Canadian Discovery and Exploration.* Toronto: Hounslow Press, 1988.
Fascinating speculation on Henry Sinclair's voyage to Nova Scotia, a pre-Columbian Nova Scotia settlement, Oak Island, and the founding of Montreal.

Bradley, Michael. *Grail Knights of North America: On the Trail of the Grail Legacy in Canada and the United States.* Toronto: Hounslow Press, 1998.
Whether or not you believe any of Bradley's theories, he is interesting reading.

Brown, Craig. *The Illustrated History of Canada.* Toronto: Key Porter Books Limited, 1997.
A thorough and readable general history of the country.

Brooks, Stephen. *Canadian Democracy: An Introduction.* 5th edition. Don Mills, Ontario: Oxford University Press, 2007.
A thorough introduction to the Canadian political system.

Bruce, Harry, and Dudley Whitney. *Atlantic Canada.* Toronto: Key Porter Books Limited, 1991.
All four Atlantic provinces in text and photographs.

Brym, Robert J., editor. *Regionalism in Canada.* Toronto: Irwin Publishing, 1986.
A scholarly treatment that includes case studies on British Columbia and Newfoundland.

Bursey, Brian C. *Discovering Newfoundland.* St. John's: Harry Cuff Publications, 1993.
A companion book to the author's earlier Labrador volume, Bursey opens up parts of Newfoundland often not experienced by even the veteran traveler.

Bursey, Brian C. *Exploring Labrador.* St. John's: Harry Cuff Publications, 1991.
A mostly photographic narrative that reveals the story of a haunting land
unfortunately known by only a few.

Campbell, Lyall. *Sable Island: Fatal and Fertile Crescent.* Hantsport, Nova
Scotia: Lancelot Press, 1974.
The history of this remote and now economically important island.

Chaput, Marcel, with translation by Robert A. Taylor. *Why I Am a
Separatist.* Toronto: The Ryerson Press, 1962.
An early discussion of the sovereignty question by a federal civil servant
from Quebec.

Communications Division of Statistics Canada. *Canada Year Book.*
Ottawa: Ministry of the Interior, published annually.
An indispensable source of economic and other statistical data.

Conlogue, Ray. *Impossible Nation: The Longing for Homeland in Canada and
Quebec.* Stratford, Ontario: The Mercury Press, 1996.
A study of the mutual misunderstandings between Quebec and Canada
and what could be done about them.

Courchene, Thomas J., with Colin R. Telmer. *From Heartland to North
American Region State: The Social, Fiscal and Federal Evolution of Ontario.*
Toronto: University of Toronto, 1998.
A very revealing study by the university's Centre for Public Management
of the economic and resulting political power of Ontario.

Crooker, William S. *Oak Island Gold.* Halifax: Nimbus Publishing Limited,
1993.
Crooker's book is among the most thorough of the numerous ones
devoted to the history of Oak Island and its possible treasure.

Dale, Ronald J. *The Invasion of Canada: Battles of the War of 1812.* Toronto:
James Lorimer & Company Limited, 2001.

A very different view of the War of 1812 from the one Americans learned in school.

DeKay, William. *Down Home: A Journey into Rural Canada.* Toronto: Stoddart Publishing Company 1997.
A beautiful photographic essay of a Canada that at least in some places may be slowly fading away.

Dyck, Rand. *Canadian Politics: Concise Second Edition.* Scarborough, Ontario: Thomson/Nelson, 2002.
A brief but thorough introduction to the Canadian political system.

Eiselt, Marianne, and H. A. Eiselt. *Discovering New Brunswick.* Halifax: Formac Publishing Limited, 2002.
A moving presentation of the people and places of the province in text and photographs.

Ferguson, Bruce, and William Pope. *Glimpses into Nova Scotia History.* Hantsport, Nova Scotia: Lancelot Press, 1974.
A brief, well-illustrated introduction to the province.

Finnan, Mark. *The Sinclair Saga.* Halifax: Formac Publishing Limited, 1999. Insights into Scottish Prince Henry Sinclair's possible 1398 voyage to Nova Scotia.

Fischer, George, and Claude Bouchard. *Destination Fundy Trail New Brunswick.* Halifax: Nimbus Publishing Limited, 2002.
The magic of the Fundy coast in text and photographs.

Flanagan, Tom. *Waiting for the Wave: The Reform Party and Preston Manning.* Toronto: Stoddart Publishing Company Limited, 1995.
An insider's examination of the rise of the Alberta-based Reform party.

Fleming, Mark. *Churchill: Polar Bear Capital of the World.* Winnipeg: Hyperion Press Limited, 1988.
In text and stunning photographs Fleming tells the story of this most unforgettable community.

Francis, Daniel. *National Dreams: Myth, Memory, and Canadian History.* Vancouver: Arsenal Pulp Press, 1997.
Fascinating, if not always flattering, insights on how Canadians have viewed themselves.

Francis, R. Douglas, Richard Jones, and Donald B. Smith. *Destinies: Canadian History Since Confederation.* Toronto: Holt, Rinehart and Winston of Canada Limited, 1988.
A good general treatment of Canada since 1867.

Friesen, Gerald. *The West: Regional Ambitions, National Debates, Global Age.* Toronto: Penguin Books, 1999.
Friesen sees a more diverse and complex Western Canada than is often observed.

Grand Council of the Crees (Eeyou Astchee). *Never Without Consent: James Bay Crees' Stand Against Forcible Inclusion into an Independent Quebec.* Toronto: ECW Press, 1998.
Fortunately relations between Quebec and the First Nations have undergone dramatic improvement since this was written, and several agreements have been made, including one with the Cree pertaining to the James Bay area. However, the book still makes a powerful case for First Nations' rights.

Hansen, Ben. *St. Pierre & Miquelon.* Halifax: Numbus Publishing Limited, 1994.
Fascinating photographic portrait of Newfoundland's French neighbor.

Hines, Sherman. *Alberta.* Halifax: Nimbus Publishing Limited, 1981.
Magnificent photographs of a magnificent province.

Hines, Sherman, with introduction by Elizabeth Pacey. *Halifax, Nova Scotia*. Halifax: Nimbus Publishing Limited, 1994.
The story of Nova Scotia's historic capital in photographs and text.

Holman, Carrie Ellen. *Our Island Story: Broadcasts Given Over CFCY Charlottetown in the Winter of 1948*. Summerside, PEI: published for the benefit of Prince County Hospital, 1991.
Local history as told by a true daughter of Prince Edward Island. Difficult to locate.

Houston, James. *Confessions of an Igloo Dweller*. Boston: Houghton Mifflin Company, 1995.
This is the moving autobiographical narrative of the man who introduced Inuit art to the world and lived among these Arctic people for fourteen years. A talented artist himself, few have known the Arctic Inuit as well as Houston and his family, and none have loved them more. Houston has also published a variety of adult and juvenile fiction based on his Arctic experiences.

Jackson, Robert J., and Doreen Jackson. *Politics in Canada: Culture, Institutions, Behaviour and Public Policy*. 3rd edition. Scarborough, Ontario: Prentice Hall Canada Incorporated, 1994.
A very thorough treatment of the Canadian political system.

Knowles, Kathleen. *A Rock and Hard Place: Impressions, reflections, reminiscences*. St. John's: Creative Publishers, 1993.
The sensitive story of a Canadian who moved to Newfoundland and found it a different world from the one she had known.

Laird, Gordon. *Slumming It at the Rodeo: The Cultural Roots of Canada's Right-Wing Revolution*. Vancouver: Douglas & McIntyre, 1998.
A sometimes controversial and critical exploration of Western conservatism.

Lipset, Seymour Martin. *Continental Divide: The Values and Institutions of the United States and Canada.* New York: Routledge, 1990.
An excellent analysis of the differences between the two peoples by a highly respected scholar.

Lloyd, Tanya. *Ontario.* Vancouver: Whitecap Books, 1997.
Photographic essay of Canada's most populous province.

McCormick, Peter, Ernest C. Manning, and Gordon Gibson. *Regional Representation: The Canadian Partnership.* Calgary: Canada West Foundation, 1981.
A Western proposal for extensive governmental reform.

Malcolm, Andrew H. *The Canadians.* New York: Times Books, 1985.
An informative and entertaining examination of the national character of the Canadian people.

McLeod, Carol. *Glimpses into New Brunswick History.* Hantsport, Nova Scotia, Lancelot Press, 1984.
A brief and readable introduction to the subject.

Marshall, Ingeborg. *The Beothuk of Newfoundland: A Vanished People.* St. John's: Breakwater Books, 1989.
The tragic story of a destroyed Indian culture.

Martin, Ged, editor. *The Causes of Canadian Confederation.* Fredericton: Acadiensis Press,1990.
Scholarly and readable essays on how and why Canada was created.

Meisel, John, Guy Rocher, and Arthur Silver, editors. *As I Recall/ Si je me souviens bien.* Montreal: Institute for Research on Public Policy, 1999.
A collection of most fascinating essays demonstrating how English and French Canadians can look at the same events and understand them quite differently.

Morris, Jan. *O Canada: Travels in an Unknown Country*. New York: HarperCollins, 1990.
Morris traveled to ten Canadian cities and towns and reveals their unique differences.

Morrison, William R. *True North: The Yukon and Northwest Territories*. Toronto: Oxford University Press, 1998.
A well illustrated, highly professional treatment of an all too often forgotten part of the country.

Mortimore, G. E. *British Columbia: A Symphony in Color*. Don Mills, Ontario: Collins Publishers, 1982.
Text and photographs of the beautiful Pacific province.

Newman, Peter C. *An Illustrated History of the Hudson's Bay Company*. Toronto: Penguin Books Canada Limited, 1995.
This edition commemorates the 325th anniversary of the world's oldest continuously operating corporation.

The Nunavut Handbook. Iqaluit, Nunavut: Nortext Multimedia Inc., published annually.
Absolutely everything you need to know whether traveling to or just interested in the Inuit Homeland.

Quebec: La Belle Province. Canada: Editions Phidal, 1995.
Text in English and French with beautiful photographs.

Pindell, Terry. *Last Train to Toronto: A Canadian Rail Odyssey*. New York: Henry Holt and Company, 1992.
A glorious exploration of this vast and diverse nation.

Reid, Scott. *Canada Remapped: How the Partition of Quebec Will Reshape the Nation.* Vancouver: Arsenal Pulp Press Limited, 1992.
After reviewing mostly European past partition plans, Reid presents an interesting proposal that is probably unacceptable to nearly everyone who would be involved.

Schledermann, Peter. *The Vikings Saga.* London: Weidenfeld & Nicholson, 1997.
A brief but excellent examination of possible contact between the Vikings and the Inuit of Canada and Greenland.

Silversides, Brock V. *Prairie Sentinel: The Story of the Canadian Grain Elevator.* Calgary: Fifth House Publishers, 1997.
Once a symbol of the prairies, the old grain elevators of Saskatchewan, Manitoba, and Alberta are rapidly disappearing to be replaced by more efficient but less romantic structures.

Smallwood, Joseph, "Joey" R. *I Chose Canada: The Memoirs of the Honourable Joseph R. "Joey Smallwood.* Toronto: Macmillan of Canada, 1973.
The man who led Newfoundland and Labrador into the Canadian Confederation tells his life story.

Thurston, Harry. *Atlantic Outposts.* Lawrencetown Beach, Nova Scotia: Pottersfield Press, 1990.
Thurston takes the reader on an unforgettable tour of remote coastal communities in the Maritimes, Newfoundland and Labrador, and Quebec.

Thurston, Harry, Wayne Barrett, and Anne MacKay. *Building the Bridge to P.E.I.* Halifax: Nimbus Publishing Limited, 1998.
The story of Confederation Bridge in text and photographs.

Tomblin, Stephen G. *Ottawa and the Outer Provinces: The Challenge of Regional Integration in Canada.* Toronto: James Lorimer & Company, 1995.
An excellent study of Canada's regional tendencies.

Wallace, Mary. *The Inuksuk Book*. Toronto: Greey de Pencier Books, 1999.
Although this is actually a children's book, adults will also find the story of the inuksuk to be a fascinating one. In a world without trees, the stone inuksuk becomes the signpost that leads the way. The book also has a brief guide to Inuktitut, the language of the Inuit.

Wellman, Jim. *The Broadcast: The Story of CBC Radio's Fisheries Broadcast*. St. John's: Creative Book Publishing, 1997.
An unusual look at the life of an unusual people, the courageous fisherman of Newfoundland.

Williams, Alan F. *John Cabot and Newfoundland*. St. John's: Newfoundland Historical Society, 1996.
A study of Cabot's controversial 1497 voyage of discovery.

Woodward, Meredith Bain. *Land of Dreams: A History in Photographs of the British Columbia Interior*. Banff and Vancouver: Altitude Publishing Canada Limited, 1993.
A skillful examination of British Columbia's past.

Zierler, Amy, and Cam Mustard. *Signal Hill: An Illustrated History*. St. John's Newfoundland Historic Parks Association, 1997.
Not only relates the story of Marconi's successful trans-Atlantic wireless transmission, but also covers the early history of St. John's and Newfoundland.

Zimmer, Robert. *Dreams Come True: Memories of a Prairie Boy*. Ocala, Florida: Sorrels Printing, 2006. Order from http://www.orchardhouse.biz
The first sixty pages of this autobiography of a Lutheran clergyman are the moving account of his early years in Saskatchewan and Alberta.

APPENDIX V
Learning Canadian French

As a tourist in Canada, even in Quebec, you can communicate quite easily in English. However, this is increasingly a bilingual country. If you know or are willing to learn a little French, you will delight the francophone speakers you encounter and probably find your journey is still more informative and fascinating. The French you learned in high school, college, or traveling about Europe is certainly satisfactory, but Canadian French over several centuries has developed some characteristics of its own. The situation is not unlike comparing British and American English. So, even if you have already studied some French you might find an examination of the Canadian variety to be of interest. If you have never studied the language you may want to start with the Canadian approach to it.

A very economical introduction to both Canadian and European French is available on Transparent Languages CD-ROM *101 Languages of the World*. This innovative program and your computer can actually help you learn the basics of over seventy-five languages plus some vocabulary for several dozen more. The cost is most reasonable, and it is easy and fun to use. In addition to teaching you elementary Canadian and European French, it will enable you to learn some helpful words in the Inuit language of Inuktitut and in Mohawk, a Canadian First Nations language.

The included word processor can even be used to write syllabics, the symbols used in written Inuktitut and in such First Nations languages as Cree.

None of this will make you fluent, but it will give you a start. The four-disk set may be on sale at book, computer, and office supply stores. It can also be obtained on the Internet (http://www.transparent.com).